Charles Henry Churchill

The Druzes and the Maronites under the Turkish Rule from 1840 to 1860

Charles Henry Churchill

The Druzes and the Maronites under the Turkish Rule from 1840 to 1860

ISBN/EAN: 9783743317055

Manufactured in Europe, USA, Canada, Australia, Japa

Cover: Foto ©ninafisch / pixelio.de

Manufactured and distributed by brebook publishing software (www.brebook.com)

Charles Henry Churchill

The Druzes and the Maronites under the Turkish Rule from 1840 to 1860

THE
DRUZES AND THE MARONITES

Under the Turkish Rule

FROM 1840 TO 1860

BY

COLONEL CHURCHILL

AUTHOR OF
"TEN YEARS' RESIDENCE IN MOUNT LEBANON, 1853"

LONDON
BERNARD QUARITCH, 15 PICCADILLY
1862

PREFACE.

ALTHOUGH some months have elapsed since the appalling intelligence of the massacres in Syria burst upon the civilised world, and although ample details were given to the public, at the time, of those heart-rending events, a full appreciation of their meaning can only be attained by a consideration of the various causes which, accumulating and gathering strength through the preceding twenty years, at last culminated in that extraordinary calamity.

Having resided in the Lebanon during nearly the whole of that period, and availed myself of my ample opportunities to fathom the pervading mind, as it were, of the two great sects into which its population is divided, I think I am peculiarly in a position to speak authoritatively, and I trust impartially, of the sentiments which inspired, and the principles which actuated them throughout that unfortunate and prolonged career of jealously and rivalry which has at last terminated in their common ruin. The result of my study and observation I now offer to the public, in the hope that it may help all who are interested in the affairs of Syria, to regulate their sympathies and direct their judgment.

My analysis of sectarian and political motives, whether Druze or Maronite, is based upon intimate and unreserved communication with both parties. My delineations of character are drawn from personal experience: I neither vindicate nor condemn. It is for the reader to draw his own conclusions.

That a government should conspire to murder its own subjects, after having deliberately disarmed them, seems a deed so inexplicably heinous as to surpass belief. Such, however, is the monstrous crime of which the Turkish Government in Syria stands both arraigned and condemned at the bar of Europe. The following pages afford the most conclusive testimony as to the intenseness and magnitude of this enormity on the part of the Turks. They show, likewise, that the policy which sanctioned their barbarities towards the native Christians, is not the offspring of unguarded and momentary impulse, but the suggestion of a spirit of calculating and deliberate malice and hatred, spreading its meshes through a long series of years, to circumvent and then trample upon its unfortunate victims.

The time is fast approaching when the imperative claims of Christianity and humanity must and ought to absorb all others in the much-vexed Eastern Question. I would fain hope that this present work may induce some to take this point of view when contemplating England's present or anticipated action in the political affairs of the Ottoman empire.

CHARLES HENRY CHURCHILL.

Beyrout, Syria.

CONTENTS.

CHAPTER I.

Retrospect of the former History of the Druzes and Maronites — The Druze Religion — Turkish and Egyptian Rule in Syria .   PAGES 1—30

CHAPTER II.

Emir Beshir Kassim — Maronite Intrigues — 1841, Affray at Deir-el-Kamar — Turkish Policy — Attack upon Zachlé . . . . . . 31—62

CHAPTER III.

1842, Omar Pasha Governor of the Lebanon — Druze Revolt — Shibli-el-Arrian — January 1, 1843, Defeat of the Druzes — The Druze and the Christian Kaimmakams — January 1845, Said Bey Jumblatt — Maronite Attack upon the Druzes — Defeat of the Christians . . 63—94

CHAPTER IV.

Survey, 1856 — Prosperity of Deir-el-Kamar, Zachlé, and Hasbeya, Christian Towns in the Druze Districts — Intolerance of the Maronite Patriarch . . 95—131

CONTENTS.

CHAPTER V.

Affray, August 1859 — Kurchid Pasha — Druze Aggression, May 1860 — Deir-el-Kamar taken — Massacre in Jezeen — June 3, 1860, appalling Slaughter of the Males at Hasbeya; and June 4, at Rascheya — Sitt Naaify (Said Bey Jumblatt's Sister), gloats over the mangled Corpses of the butchered Christians . . . PAGES 132—173

CHAPTER VI.

June 11, 1860, the Massacre at Kanakin by Ismail-il-Uttrush — June 14, Zachlé invested and taken — June 19, the Slaughter of the Male Population at Deir-el-Kamar.
174—206

CHAPTER VII.

July 9, 1860, the Mohammedans of Damascus rise upon the Christians — Huge Deluge of Massacre and Fire — Abd-el-Kader saves 12,000 Christians — Statistics of the Massacres — August 3, Conference of the European Powers at Paris . . . . 207—221

CHAPTER VIII.

Peace — July 17, 1860, Fuad Pasha — August 16, a French Division of 7000 men arrives — Mock Trials of Druze Prisoners — Turkish Treachery and Druze Ferocity remain unpunished — June 5, 1861, Departure of the French Troops . . . . . 222—254

CHAPTER IX.

October 5, 1860 to March 5, 1861, fruitless Results of the Meetings of the European Commission — Lord Dufferin's noble Efforts. — The Slaughter of 5000 human Beings remains unpunished — Triumph of Turkish Duplicity — Appeal to Christian Europe for Justice . 255—283

THE DRUZES AND THE MARONITES.

CHAPTER I.

Turkish Jealousy of the Native Christian Races. — Impossibility of Turkish Regeneration. — Revival of old Mohammedan Antipathies. — Fanaticism of the Turks. — False Position of the Rayahs. — Retrospect of the former History of the Druzes and the Maronites. — The Druzes of the Lebanon in the Eleventh Century. — Hakem, Neshtakeen Darazi, and Hamzé, the Founders of the two Druze Sects. — Cabalistic Language. — The Ockals and Djahels. — The Druzes during the Middle Ages. — Early History of the Maronites. — Turkish Rule. — Egyptian Rule.

To Europeans residing in the Ottoman empire, who come in daily contact with the Turkish authorities, and who have thereby the opportunities of watching and analysing the general course of their internal policy, the frightful scenes which have lately occurred in Syria are but the natural results of that persistent jealousy of the native Christian races which has long been, and ever will be, a predominant feature in the character of the Turk.

It is of no use assuring *them* that the Porte is anxious to battle with the religious prejudices and time-honoured convictions of its Mohammedan subjects,— convictions which oppose an insurmountable barrier to the extinction of those marks of inferiority which still affect the rayahs; and that it earnestly wishes to carry out administrative reforms based on the principles of an enlightened religious toleration. *They* know but too well that such assurances are mere moonshine; that such expectations, albeit entertained and even paraded by a certain school of statesmen and diplomatists, are utterly nugatory and fallacious; and that all the Hati-Scheriffs and Hati-Homayooms, with their accompanying cortége of Special Commissions, Imperial letters, and letters Vizierial, which the Porte from time to time flaunts with such ostentation in the face of the world, are but so many tubs thrown out to the great European whale, ever following in its wake and threatening to engulf it.

Experience quickly dissipates the most fondly

cherished ideas of the possibility of Turkish regeneration, in the European sense of the word, and recent events were hardly required to convince even the most sanguine philo-Turk, that every year gained for the existence of the Ottoman empire, in its present aspect, from the jealous forbearance of the European powers, is only just so much obtained for the continuance of one of the most singular systems of political importance which was ever foisted on the credulity of mankind.

This strange anomaly, joint compound of mongrel liberality and rampant fanaticism, owes its ill-omened conception, its monstrous birth, and its lugubrious vitality, to that political connection and affinity with the Christian states which constantly impels the Porte to make, or rather to have the semblance of making, the utterly futile and incongruous attempt of harmonising and blending the hostile and divergent systems of Mohammedanism and Christianity. The universal heart of Islam scornfully repudiates and abhors such an alliance. Hitherto, history has invariably taught, that these religions can only exist together in the mutual relation of the conquering and the conquered.

Hence, while the Sultan and his ministers, in order to meet the exigencies of their position, outwardly profess the most advanced theories of civil and religious equality, they dare not, for fear of alarming the religious susceptibilities of his orthodox followers, enforce any measures for giving them fair play and efficiency. Nay, more, whether with his consent or not, it is indisputable that within the last few years, doctrines emanating from the Porte itself, have been actively propagated throughout his empire, encouraging all true believers to the assumption of an attitude towards the rayahs, not only inimical, but openly defiant.

Nor is it hard to divine the animus which more particularly inspires the Turks in this attempted revival of the old Mohammedan antipathies. Pride of race and pride of religion have ever been their distinguishing characteristics. They instinctively feel that the full-blown doctrines of religious toleration, which the European powers are forcing upon their acceptance, if once allowed to obtain strength and currency in their territories, will lay the sap to that exclusive and domineering ascendancy which they regard as pre-eminently theirs by right of conquest. They foresee that the practical admission of the rayahs to common rights and privileges with themselves, will slowly, perhaps, but assuredly, conduct them to that vantage ground, which superior intelligence, industry, and activity, invariably secure to its possessors. They regard with sullen distrust the *status* which these once humble, crouching, and submissive rayahs have been lately acquiring in their dominions.

They see them hopeful, innovating, and ambitious, displaying a confidence almost tantamount to daring. They know that these aggressive tendencies proceed not so much from their own powers of combination as from extraneous and adventitious circumstances; and, viewing them doubly armed with the menacing and portentous adjuncts of foreign religious sympathy and foreign political prestige, they dread them and they hate them.

It was consequently to be expected that the Turks would seek, by every means in their power, to check what they consider the further encroachments of sectarians thus countenanced and thus stimulated: that they would, by slippery devices, by evasions, by hypocrisy, by every species of fraud and artifice, endeavour to shirk the fulfilment of whatever promises might have been extorted from them in behalf of the rayahs, by their Christian allies. Had they restrained themselves to such a course of proceeding, relying on the efficacy of plausible subterfuge, and the strength of diplomatic effrontery to compass their ends, it is highly probable they might have eventually succeeded in wearing out and altogether nullifying the efforts of European interference. Ambassadorial and consular representations, by being adroitly and perseveringly eluded, would have been gradually disarmed of their strength and efficacy, and to almost any distant period the Turks might have continued to play off their cameleon-like policy without let or hindrance, and to entangle the brightest intellects of Christendom in the intricacies of their plausible finesse.

The late atrocious proceedings, however, in Syria,— supported, countenanced, and abetted, as they undoubtedly were, by the first dignitaries in the empire, — have placed the Turks in such a detestable point of view, — have so clearly and unmistakeably evinced the savage propensities which still lurk in their nature, — have so terrifically revealed their unmitigated hatred to our common Christianity, — that all further patience with them is felt to be not only superfluous but absolutely criminal; and outraged religion, humanity and civilisation alike demand the adoption of some such measures by the powers of Europe as may show these semi-barbarians that there exists both the will and the power to curb their presumptuous and bloody fanaticism, and to make them feel that not even in Mecca itself can the Mohammedan slay, or oppress, or insult a Christian without incurring the full weight of a swift and adequate retribution.

The Christian states of Europe have, by common consent, assumed the right of superintending and watching over the welfare of their co-religionists in the Turkish empire, — a right fully warranted by the imprescriptible sanction and requirements of religious duty and political conservation. But to accomplish this end, it is not merely by offering advice to, or eliciting promises from, the Porte that any real or permanent advantage and security can be obtained for the rayahs. Barely to announce such a right in that quarter is simply to hand it over to mockery and derision. Experience uniformly shows that the Turks are hypocritical, evasive and fanatic.

The utterly absurd and fatuitous, nay dangerous, principle of "non-intervention," which the British Government, in a moment of misplaced confidence, was the first to enounce in its relations with the Porte, must be at once and for ever abandoned; for to it may be primarily ascribed all the conspiracies, the crimes, and the horrors of which Syria has lately been the scene. All false delicacy on this point must be repudiated; otherwise, whatever reforms may be promulgated, or whatever assurances given by the Porte for the ostensible benefit of the rayahs, will remain, as they have hitherto done, so many dead letters, not only impotent for good, but directly productive of the greatest misery to the very class on whose behalf they may have been enunciated.

For, while, on the one hand, the rayahs will be induced, in reliance on them, to aspire to a position which they will not only never attain, but the very attempt to attain which will draw upon them the jealousy and hatred of every local authority, with all its consequent evils and calamities; the Turks, on the other, finding themselves unquestioned and irresponsible in the exercise of their power over them, will take a malicious pleasure in making them feel the shallowness and uselessness of those foreign sympathies on which they so fondly depend, and in expiating on their unfortunate heads the humiliating dictation to which, for their sakes, they had been obliged to submit.

If, then, the European powers feel that they have the right to elicit promises from the Porte as regards the rayahs, they must, if they wish to be consistent, — if they have any regard for their own dignity, — if they wish their sympathy for the rayahs to be productive of any, even the slightest good, — if they wish, in fact, not to be stultified, —

insist also on having the right to name representatives throughout the Ottoman empire, authorised and entitled to see that those promises are fulfilled.

That various antecedent causes have contributed to bring about the late awful catastrophe in Syria, is unquestionable. To be thoroughly understood, it must be viewed in different points of view, and extenuating circumstances may, perhaps, be found for some at least of the parties engaged in the dreadful struggle. As this subject cannot be said to possess merely a passing interest,—as the effects of this awful exhibition of human wickedness and malignity will make themselves felt in various channels, permanently affecting the future political condition, and even, perhaps, the social standing of some of the different sects which exist in Syria, —a brief retrospect of the former history of the two sects who were prominent actors in the late events, as well as of their relations with the Turks, will be found somewhat conducive to a proper appreciation of the stirring theme.

The sect of the Druzes is first heard of in the Lebanon, about the beginning of the eleventh century. One of the Arab tribes, which had settled there two centuries before, furnished proselytes to a certain Neshtakeen Darazi, a missionary, who had been sent into Syria by Hamzé, the vizier of Hakem, the Fatimite Caliph then reigning in Egypt,—to preach the doctrine of the divinity of that successor of Ali. The sect of the Batenians, or believers in the hidden meaning of the Koran, which had already obtained great power and influence in the eighth century, inculcated the belief that Ali and his successors in the caliphate were eminently impregnated with the divine essence. Hamzé, one of its chief ulemas, merely pushed the doctrine to its extreme limits, by teaching that the existing caliph, Hakem, was an incarnation of the divinity itself. Such was the tenet he launched forth into the Eastern world. It obtained adherents in various parts, —in Morocco, in Persia, in Syria, and even in India. Neshtakeen Darazi, armed by Hamzé with apostolic powers, succeeded in gathering around him a certain number of followers accepting this doctrine in a small district lying between the Lebanon and Anti-Lebanon, called Wady-el-Tame.

Darazi, elated by his success, assumed the airs of a pontiff; declared himself head of the sect, and, in order to obtain converts, sanctioned the most licentious principles. Hamzé, indignant at his treachery and rebellion, formally deposed him from his functions, denounced him emphatically, as the "Calf," whom a deluded people had set up as their idol, and contrived at length to have him assassinated by the Druzes themselves in Wady-el-Tame. The disciple whom Hamzé sent to replace him was named Moktana Baha-edeen. He it was who may be said to have placed the Druze religion on the basis on which it at present stands. His numerous tracts and epistles have ever been the chief subjects of study and contemplation in the Druze Holorvés.

Nevertheless, the teaching of Darazi was too seducing in its tendency to be ever entirely abandoned by many who had once reconciled themselves to a system of theology, which, under the imposing epithet of the mysteries, threw a cloak over the indulgence of the worst passions of human nature. The schism was never eradicated; and to this day the Druzes are divided into two sects, who, although bound together in a common faith in the Hakem and Hamzé, are actuated respectively, in their conduct, by the purer and more orthodox moral and religious teaching of Baha-edeen, or by the dark and unscrupulous libertinism of Darazi. The former, it is but just to say, form a great majority; the latter are ever ready for the indulgence and committal of every kind of lust and atrocity.

Darazi, however, exercised his authority for a sufficient number of years to enable him to stamp his name on the sect which first arose under his auspices; and to this circumstance it is owing, that all the followers of the doctrines preached by Hamzé, instead of being called Hamzéites, as might and ought to have been the case, are called Druzes.

During the Crusades the Druzes were noticed by more than one contemporary writer, as a sect "secretly devoted to the worship of the Calf, eating pork, and given to licentious practices." They were, at that time, already bound together under the singular form of theocracy by which they are at present distinguished. The doctrine of the divinity of Hakem, asserted by Hamzé, had been scouted in Cairo from its first enunciation. Hamzé's temporary absence from his post, and Darazi's mission to the Lebanon, were the immediate consequences of this unfortunate essay. After Hakem's death, in A.D. 1025, Hamzé, consulting his own safety, disappeared altogether: by some thought to have been murdered, by others to have fled into the desert. The Druzes still look forward to his reappearance in China, as a mighty conqueror, leading on his faithful followers to victory, dominion, and glory; for it is their firm belief that their sect exists in the interior of China at the present moment, in overwhelming numbers.

The successor of Hakem adopted the most searching and rigorous measures for the extirpation of the odious heresy. A decree of extirmination was issued against all who had accepted it, throughout Egypt and Syria. In the fastnesses of the Lebanon alone, the sectarians contrived to enjoy a comparative security. Yet even there their meetings were held in secluded places, and were conducted with the greatest caution and reserve. A cabalistic language was adopted for mutual recognition, in case of an obligatory dispersion. To these stealthy and hazardous reunions, none were admitted but those whose character indicated them to be entirely trustworthy, and capable of implicit secresy. A long trial and probation at last became necessary, ere even professing believers were allowed to join the favoured ranks. Hence the classes of the Ockals or initiated, and the Djahels or ignorant, into which the Druzes are divided. Outwardly, the entire sect professed the formulas and practised the ceremonies of orthodox Islamism.

To a sect thus reduced to the defensive, and ever painfully and laboriously concealing its existence, the idea of any further proselytism was clearly impossible. Whatever successes its teachers had obtained, had been acquired during the preaching of Darazi and Baha-edeen, extending over a period of less than thirty years. The latter, on his dying bed, declared the world to be unworthy of the marvellous grace which had been offered to it at the hands of the divine Hakem and the transcendant Hamzé, and enjoined his disciples to cease altogether from seeking to gain over a generation which only repaid their efforts with contumely and reproach. The work of conversion from this time ceased. The door of salvation was declared to be closed. The Druze religion became an hereditary privilege, a sacred deposit, a priceless treasure, to be jealously guarded from profane curiosity. The Druzes henceforward acquired strength and importance, simply by their own increasing numbers.

As the great Arab tribe of Beni Tuhnooch had more or less adopted the doctrines of Hamzé, so we find it, till about the middle of the twelfth century, exclusively supplying the great chiefs who regulated the temporal affairs of the Druzes. Their castles crowned the most commanding sites in the Lebanon. Numerous Druze villages, thickly populated, extended over all its southern ranges, exhibiting a general aspect of prosperity.

During the Crusades, the Druzes furnished a respectable contingent to the Mussulman ranks. In the fifteenth century they rose to the height of their power, and occupied the towns of Beyrout and Sidon. The Mohammedan family of Maan had been introduced among them, and invested with feudal jurisdiction by Sultan Nouradeen, and, finally, even supplanted the Tuhnooch emirs in their hitherto exclusive ascendancy. The religion of their rulers has never been an obstacle to allegiance amongst the Druzes, so long as no attempts are made to coerce their own belief, or to abridge their privileges. Mohammedans, Metualis and Christians, alike found perfect security and complete toleration amongst them. They paid their tribute through the medium of commissioners, sent down from time to time to collect it; and it was not till the eighteenth century, that the Porte endeavoured to subject them to the direct control of Turkish pashas.

While the Druzes were thus prosperously establishing their power as a community in the southern portions of the Lebanon, and with such repute, that the entire range obtained the generic appellation of the Mountain of the Druzes, its northern portions were inhabited and brought into the highest state of cultivation by the Christian sect of the Maronites.

Nicephorus, in his ecclesiastical history, states

that the Maronites were originally a Monothelite sect, founded by the monk Maron, who built and lived in a convent on the banks of the Orontes, near Hamah, in the seventh century: a testimony fully corroborated by William of Tyre and Jacques de Vitry. The latter was Bishop of Acre in the twelfth century, and in his "Historia Hierosolymitana," drawn up at the request of Pope Honorius III., says:—"Men armed with bows and arrows, and skilful in battle, inhabit the mountains in considerable numbers, in the province of Phœnicia, not far from the town of Biblos. They are called Maronites, from the name of a certain man, their master, Maron, a heretic, who affirmed that there was in Jesus but one will or operation. The Christians of the Lebanon, dupes of this diabolical error of Maron, remained separate from the Church nearly five hundred years. At last, their hearts being turned, they made profession of the Catholic faith in presence of the venerable Father Amaury, Patriarch of Antioch, and adopted the traditions of the Holy Roman Church." It was not, however, till the close of the fifteenth century, that the Maronite clergy consented to acknowledge the supremacy of the Pope in matters of ecclesiastical discipline. This point was carried by Eugenius IV. A.D. 1438.

After the final expulsion of the Franks from Syria by Malek Ashraf, A.D. 1300, the Maronites had to defend their independence against the repeated attacks of the Mameluke sovereigns of Egypt. Though never completely subdued, numbers from time to time sought repose and safety in foreign lands. Some settled in Cyprus, others faithful to the standard of the Hospitallers, followed that order to Candia and Sicily; while not a few found a nearer place of refuge amongst the Druzes. The Greek Christians had been located in the Druze districts from the very commencement of the Druze nationality, and are to this day looked upon by the Druzes with feelings almost of fraternity, and considered as indispensably incorporated with their political existence.

Throughout their various trials and adversities, the Maronites never ceased to keep up active relations with the Vatican, and through it contrived to obtain a certain hold on, and connection with, the Christian powers of Europe. But it was not till the seventeenth century, that their temporal affairs obtained the special care and supervision of the French government. Both Louis XIV. and Louis XV. granted them "Letters of Protection," the language of which seems to indicate that their right to do so had been more or less conceded by the Sultan. The pretended ignorance, indeed, the official denial of this right, by M. Drouyn de Llhuys in 1854, in a despatch to the Earl of Clarendon, to answer a temporary purpose, is one of the most flagrant instances of diplomatic evasion on record. The French consular authorities at Beyrout exercise a direct and almost sovereign power over the Maronite clergy, who, on their part, make no scruple of boasting of their allegiance to France, and of declaring the Maronites to be the French of the east.

About the beginning of the eighteenth century, the family of Maan having become extinct, the Druzes summoned to the government of Mount Lebanon the Mohammedan family of Shehab, a branch of the Beni Koreish, and allied by blood and marriage with the line of the Prophet, the Shehab emirs had held extended sway in the Houran ever since the taking of Damascus by their ancestor Khalid, surnamed the "Sword of God." Sultan Nouradeen gave them the petty principality of Hasbeya and Rascheya in the anti-Lebanon, in the twelfth century. Long experience of the Druze character rendered them peculiarly fitted to conciliate and govern that remarkable people; and for a long series of years their popularity amongst them was unbounded.

The year 1713 was one remarkable for the first attempt made by the Turks to make the Druzes submit to the direct rule of a pasha. Though the Turks had managed to sow dissensions amongst the mountaineers, and to obtain a certain party to their side, the attempt was successfully resisted: and the Druzes, headed by the Emir Heider Shehab, effectively taught the Turkish authorities, in the sanguinary and decisive battle of Aindara, that it was in vain for them to endeavour to establish a direct ascendancy in the Lebanon.

The feudal system of the Druzes was placed by

the Emir Heider, at this time, upon the footing on which it continued to stand until lately abolished by Fuad Pasha. The five Druze houses of Jumblatt, Abou Nakad, Abd-el-Melik, Amad and Talhook, had the jurisdiction of the southern part of the Lebanon divided amongst them. Its chief town was Deir-el-Kamar, the residence of the emir, and one of the scenes of the late massacres.

In the year 1756 an event occurred which subsequently gave rise to an entire change in the amicable relations which had hitherto existed between the Druzes and Christians, and influenced not only the fortunes of the Shehabs, but of the Lebanon itself. Two of the Shehab emirs were in that year converted to Christianity, and became Maronites. Several other emirs in the course of a few years followed the example. Though not daring openly to avow their change of faith, the effects of the ambitious policy of the Maronite clergy, or the general conduct of the Shehabs, became, at length, in an evil hour for them, unmistakably conspicuous: thus paving the way for that general disruption of the social system in the Lebanon, which has recently been consummated in such awful and revolting characters.

Though the Turks had hitherto failed in bringing the Lebanon under their direct rule and supremacy, yet the Turkish pashas of Damascus and Acre lost no means or opportunities of securing partizans amongst its emirs and sheiks, and of thus exciting rival animosities amongst them.

At this period it was under the indirect government of the Pasha of Acre, from whom its ruling prince received his investiture, and to whom the latter paid an annual tribute. The famous Djezzar, who governed that pashalick for more than thirty years, including the latter part of the eighteenth and the beginning of the nineteenth centuries, far exceeded all his predecessors in those diabolical arts which degrade and corrupt a people, by extinguishing in them all sense of self-respect, and making them fawning supplicants for courtly favour.

Partly from fear, partly from petty ambition, numbers of the feudal aristocracy of the Lebanon bowed submissively to his mandates, and rendered themselves subservient to his schemes and machinations. Indeed, Djezzar may be said to have inaugurated that unscrupulous and unprincipled policy of the Turks, which is continued to this very hour, of keeping the Lebanon in a constant state of weakness and paralysis. To attain this end, all means, however immoral or outrageous, are, in their eyes, perfectly legitimate.

Ever since the conquest of Syria by the Turks, under Sultan Selim 1521, its mountain ranges have ever more or less exercised a virtual independence. The ruler of the Lebanon, if able and enterprising, might at any time have made his influence felt throughout their whole extent. The Emir Fakaradeen Maan swayed with almost sovereign power from Antioch to Gaza. The Lebanon is, in fact, a *point d'appui*, a nucleus around which the various mountain tribes naturally congest. Should, therefore, its population ever be bound together by feelings of mutual trust and confidence, the danger to the supremacy of the Porte would be imminent. North and south of it live tribes, such as the Kurds, the Anserians, the Metualis, whose inmost sentiments towards the Turks are those of absolute hatred, and who would be only too ready to renounce their allegiance, were a native power once to arise, displaying signs of force and permanency. The mutual jealousy and dislike, however, which animates them, has hitherto sufficed to prevent such a consummation; and the policy of the Ottoman Turks is simply to foment and keep up this self-consuming fire.

In the Lebanon, at the time of which we are now speaking, the fanning of religious animosities was as yet impracticable: the Druzes and Christians lived together in the most perfect harmony and good-will. During whatever civil troubles took place amongst them, under the Tuhnoo*chs*, the Maans, and the Shehabs (and they were frequent and ever desolating), the Druzes and Christians ranged themselves promiscuously on rival sides, and were animated solely by the spirit of party. The Emir Beshir Shehab, whose long and agitated career extended from 1789 to 1840, though secretly a Maronite, never entertained, for instance, the wild idea of rallying the Maronites in a crusade against the Druzes. On the contrary, he felt the Druzes to be the most important element of his power. Though constantly at variance, and sometimes at open war with some of their leading sheiks, he always took care to have a strong Druze force in his own ranks, headed by men of weight and influence; while he never once in his whole life called for reinforcements or aid of any kind from the Maronites.

The situation and general condition of the Christians, therefore, amongst the Druzes, and indeed amongst all the mountain tribes, was, up to this period, as satisfactory as could be expected in a Mohammedan state. The Druzes, indeed, prized their Christian tenants more than those of their own sect, as being more industrious, active, and intelligent in agricultural matters; their chief men of confidence were Christians. The Christians had become themselves holders of landed property, had built villages, and erected churches and convents without the slightest opposition. They took a part in all the Druze sports. Many were excellent horsemen. Some were even possessors of considerable wealth; altogether presenting a striking contrast to the condition of their co-religionists in the great towns and on the plains.

These were, unfortunately for them, in the hands of the Turks. Turkish pashas in Aleppo, Damascus, Acre, Jerusalem,—Turkish mutsellims and agas in the smaller districts and in the petty towns along the sea-coast, exhibited all the pride of their race, and exhaled the afflatus of their supercilious and domineering fanaticism over the degraded rayahs, unchecked and unquestioned. The Christians were certainly allowed to live, for life could not lawfully be taken from them. They paid the tribute. Consequently, there were not in those days, nor could there be, any massacres. But in every other respects they were covered with scorn and humiliation. If they were suspected of having money, they were forthwith robbed. If accused of secreting treasure, bastinadoed till they confessed. A Christian was not permitted to ride, even a donkey. When meeting a Turk in the bazaar, it was his duty to give him the wall and go himself into the kennel. He dared not elevate his voice in talking with him. His apparel and his turban were black. He could not have his seal engraved in Arabic, that language being too noble for his usage; his name was engraved in Hebrew or Greek. If his house was noticed as being higher than that of his Mohammedan neighbour, it was pulled down. His corpse might not be carried by the door of a mosque.

To avoid the continual oppressions to which they were daily exposed, the Christians sought the patronage and protection of respectable and influential Mohammedans, propitiating them by presents of various kinds, and even by the performance of menial services. On these terms they were allowed to breathe the air of heaven, and were thankful.

In 1831, Syria passed under the dominion of Mohammad Ali, and his son, Ibrahim Pasha, was commissioned by him to carry out and enforce those measures which distinguished his general policy. But against all his endeavours to raise and ameliorate the condition of the Christians, the stoutest resistance was everywhere displayed.

In all the towns, the old Mohammedan families banded together and conspired to reject or nullify his decrees and ordinances. Ibrahim, however, made short work with them. After the battle of Nezib had laid Syria at his feet, his soldiers entered the principal centres of disaffection; some scores of heads of an indiscriminate crew of agas, effendis, and even cadis, were ruthlessly struck off; a deadly terror was infused throughout the land, and the emancipation of the rayahs was accomplished.

Christians were admitted into the local councils. Their evidence, before mixed tribunals of Christian and Mussulman, was valid. All distinction of dress was abolished. As secretaries, as local governors, even as military officers, in all departments of the State their services were accepted and rewarded. Numbers, who had for years been hiding themselves up in the mountains amongst the Druzes, to escape the tyrannous exactions of Djezzar and of Abdallah Pasha, returned to the sea-coast towns, and recommenced their commercial business. A brisk trade with

European merchants was quickly opened, and the harbour of Beyrout, in particular, soon became thronged with the shipping of London and Marseilles.

CHAP. II.

Egyptian Conscription.—Insurrections.—Egyptian Rule ended.
—Re-establishment of the Ottoman Rule.—Emir Beshir
Kassim.—The Irlām of the Maronite Patriarch.—Maronite
Presumption, Intolerance, and Intrigues.—An Affray at
Deir-el-Kamar, 1841.—The Druzes burn the Outskirts
of Deir-el-Kamar.—Colonel Rose saves Deir-el-Kamar.
—Victory of the Druzes.—Moderation of Naaman Bey
Jumblatt.—Emir Beshir a Prisoner.—Turkish Policy.—
Nejib Pasha.—Attack upon Zachlé.

To a people so long accustomed as the Syrians to the languid, loose and disorderly rule of the Turks, the vigorous administration of Ibrahim Pasha might well appear a tyranny. The spirit of insurrection consequently was not slow in manifesting itself. Yet it was not so much against his fiscal regulations as against his demand for a conscription that the popular mind was excited. However the Turks may have drained their resources, they had never taken away their sons, and on this point they were peculiarly sensitive. But these insurrectionary movements were uniformly abortive. All the different mountain tribes in succession were made to kiss the master hand. The Druzes were about the last to feel the dire consequences of unsuccessful rebellion.

For a long time they had gallantly maintained the unequal struggle. At length, starved out of their strongholds in the Houran, they had managed to straggle back to the Lebanon, where for some time they kept up a desultory warfare with the Egyptian forces. The latter at last, by a well-combined movement, surrounded and defeated them. The Druze insurrection thus effectually quelled, the task of Ibrahim Pasha became comparatively easy, and there can be no doubt that an efficient organisation would have ere long made Syria, in his hands, a well-ordered and flourishing province.

The Druzes, during the latter period of their revolt, had sent messengers to the purely Maronite districts, urging the Maronites to join them. Promises of aid had been freely given, but with that want of combination which generally distinguishes any attempt at union amongst the tribes, the Christians did not begin to move until after the Druzes had been finally overthrown. To justify their insurrection they exhibited a list of grievances, mostly imaginary, and none of any importance, save the fact, that the officers of Ibrahim Pasha used occasionally to seize their mules, and take a certain number of villagers against their will to work at a coal mine which had been lately opened in the Lebanon. A more absurd and unjustifiable motive for rebellion cannot be conceived; for both the peasants and the hire of the mules were punctually paid. The rising was isolated, and soon put down. The leaders were seized and sent into exile in Egypt.

At this very juncture, in the summer of 1840, the allied fleets of England, Austria and Turkey appeared off the coast, summoning the Syrians to return to their allegiance to the Sultan. The expiring embers of the Maronite insurrection were eagerly fanned and put into a blaze by Turkish agents, some of whom were Englishmen; and the general effervescence soon furnished ample materials for long reports as to the grievous tyranny under which the Christians of the Lebanon were groaning, and the delight with which they welcomed the English as their deliverers. Mohammad Ali found it useless to struggle against the combined powers of Europe, deserted as he was by the French, who had all along buoyed up his hopes; and in less than six months, Syria was given over to the Porte.

The Turks returned like screeching vultures to their baffled prey. Every kind of appointment was openly put up to auction. All places of trust were filled up with men notorious for their cupidity and fanaticism. Justice, which during the Egyptian rule had been purified of her defilements, became again contaminated with the offal of corruption. The Christians were everywhere reviled and insulted; in many places were assaulted in the bazaars; had their turbans torn off their heads, and compelled to resume their old distinctive garb of degradation. Emissaries were sent into the mountains to excite dissensions and religious antipathies, lest the heavy and unwonted custom-house duties, exacted from the peasantry at the entrance of all the towns, might create a spirit of union and resistance.

Several native Christian merchants, who dreaded

the return of the days of Djezzar, sought and obtained the protection of European consuls. A general panic seized the rayahs, and all commercial transactions were temporarily paralysed. Fortunately there were British officers stationed throughout the country, whose reports on these proceedings were forwarded to Constantinople; and there the energetic interference and remonstrance of Lord Stratford de Redcliffe at once checked the retrograde movement.

The government of the Lebanon attracted the first attention of the Porte and its allies. The former wished to have it placed under the administration of a Turkish pasha, as more conducive to the maintenance of its direct authority, — an object which it has never lost sight of during all the changes and troubles which have since occurred. The British Government, on the contrary, with a just deference to the usages and predilections of the mountaineers, supported the nomination of an emir from the house of Shehab; the more so, as it was hoped that, under a Christian governor, the welfare of the Christians would be permanently secured. The old Emir Beshir,—who had been prevented, on the first summons sent him to return to his allegiance, partly through inclination and partly owing to the fact of his sons being actually in the service of Ibrahim Pasha, from submitting to the Sultan,—shortly afterwards surrendered, and was exiled to Malta. The late Emir Beshir Kassim Shehab was installed into the vacant dignity of Grand Prince of the Lebanon.

The Druzes viewed this appointment with a misgiving too fully justified by subsequent events. The tyrannical conduct of the old Emir Beshir towards their sect, during the latter period of his rule, had caused them to look upon the Shehabs with absolute aversion. Three of their principal families,— the Jumblatts, the Amads, and the Abou Nakads,—he had entirely ruined, destroying their abodes, confiscating their properties, draughting some of their sheiks into the ranks of the Egyptian army, and compelling others to pass their lives in exile.

All these on their return naturally saw, with dread and apprehension, the resumption of power by a member of the Shehab family. Still, had the commonest consideration, or the least display of tact been evinced towards them, there cannot be a doubt that they might easily have been won over to a cheerful compliance with an arrangement which had received the sanction of the Sultan and of the European powers. Unfortunately, the character and proceedings of their new ruler were such as violently to inflame their animosities, and to awaken in their minds, not only a painful recollection of all their past indignities, but a gloomy foreboding as to their future treatment.

Haughty, arrogant, supercilious, and fancying himself able to carry out the iron policy of his predecessor, the Emir Beshir Kassim seemed to take a delight in insulting all the Druze sheiks who came into his presence. He constantly menaced them with a deprivation of their feudal privileges, declared his intention not to leave a Druze sheik or the son of a Druze sheik in the possession of even the shadow of authority, and to distribute the Druze feudal districts amongst the members of his own family. If the Druzes were surprised and excited at seeing the arm of the civil power thus raised against them, not less was their wonder and indignation evoked when, subsequently, the ecclesiastical power of a rival sect was boldly and presumptuously put forth to reduce them to an absolute dependence and inferiority.

The Maronite patriarch, at this juncture, unscrupulously assumed to himself the right of issuing a decree curtailing, and indeed nullifying, the most important elements of the Druze polity. He sent round a circular, called the "Irlām," to the Christians of the Lebanon, in which he ordered the inhabitants of every village to write and sign a bond, by which they engaged themselves to appoint two men, who were to act as agents of each town or village, and in whom was to be vested the power always hitherto employed by the Druze sheiks alone; a scheme which, if carried into effect, would have entirely superseded and overthrown the ancient and hereditary Druze feudal rights in the mountains. Yet was this the scheme, — it may be almost said of conquest, — to achieve which the patriarch and his colleagues were already prepared to draw the sword.

Colonel Rose, in his despatches states in unqualified terms that "the Maronite clergy show a determination to uphold their supremacy in the mountains at the risk of a civil war." Civil war! — ominous words, too sadly to be realised in those oft-recurring paroxysms of blood and conflagration; which, from this epoch, and from this aggression as a primal cause, exhibit the history of the Lebanon to our view, during a series of twenty years, as the gradual development of one dark and continuous tragedy.

A more unwarrantable and irritating aggression cannot be conceived. The Druzes had hitherto done nothing, either by their language or their conduct, to justify a measure so wholly gratuitous and unprecedented. In the town of Deir-el-Kamar, which had for ages past been a feudal appanage of the Abou-Nakads, the "Irlām" was received by the Christians with singing and firing, and every token of triumphant exultation; while the Druze sheiks surveyed with astonishment from the windows of their palace a demonstration which pretended to announce to them that their power had passed away. The Emir Beshir, at the same time, instigated by the patriarch, ordered the Druzes to dismiss the Protestant schools which had been opened in their villages. Foreseeing the inevitable consequences of such proceedings, Naaman Bey Jumblatt went in person to the Maronite patriarch, and implored him to withdraw his obnoxious mandate. He was met with evasive answers, while, within his hearing, the Bishop of Beyrout boasted, that ere long the Maronites would drive the Druzes out of the country.

It is unquestionable that about this time the patriarch received no less than 20,000*l.* from France, as the sinews of war, to enable him to carry out his views, if necessary, by force. Thus thrown on the defensive, the Druzes, with their wonted activity and power of combination, began to take measures for self-preservation. With such feelings on both sides, it was clear that a collision was merely a question of time.

Not content with thus exciting dissensions and animosities between his co-religionists and the Druzes, the patriarch, with an incomprehensible fatuity, acted in such a manner as to draw down upon him the displeasure, and excite the jealousy, of the Turkish authorities. The question as to the annual tribute to be paid to the Sultan, had for many months been warmly canvassed amongst the leaders of the Christian mountaineers. The Druzes had promptly complied with the Imperial propositions on this head, hoping, by their ready acquiescence, to obtain the sanction of the Porte to a petition they were preparing to send to Constantinople, asking to be governed either by a Druze chief or a Turkish pasha. The patriarch, on the contrary, used all his influence to excite disaffection amongst the Maronites, giving them false and exaggerated ideas of their strength and importance, misleading them as to the extent of their grievances, and making them assume almost an attitude of defiance and rebellion.

During the latter part of the administration of the old Emir Beshir, the Maronite patriarch and his clergy had acquired an influence and ascendancy most flattering to their aspirations. The emir, at their dictation, had sternly prohibited anything tending to religious toleration. The early efforts of Protestant missionaries were promptly crushed. Any one who was known to hold intercourse of any kind with Englishmen or Americans was immediately put under the ban of excommunication. The idea was sedulously impressed on the minds of the Christians, that the English were freemasons and infidels, and as such, outcasts from the Holy Catholic and Apostolic Church. On the arrival of the British fleet off the coast in 1840, a decree was issued through the mountain, that whoever went down to look on the ships should have his eyes put out. Every means that ecclesiastical ingenuity could invent was put into motion, to prevent the ingress of English ideas, political or religious, amongst the native Christian communities.

The fall of the Emir Beshir suddenly broke the hold which the Maronite clergy had thus obtained over the civil power. Though his successor, as far as he himself was concerned, showed himself perfectly willing to be their tool, yet the mere presence of the English on Syrian soil had broken the spell. The Druzes, always ready to court a dominant party, and believing, or pretending to believe, that Hamzé had his followers in England, received the English wherever they appeared, with absolute enthusiasm. They offered them the symbols of paternity. They clamorously asked for the opening of schools amongst them. They wanted to be taught, enlightened and civilised.

Hence the bitter hatred and animosity, the ebullitions of fury and excitement in which the Maronite patriarch and his clergy now constantly indulged, against the Druzes. Hence their determination at any risk to maintain, if possible, their grasp on the mixed districts, where the Druze chiefs held a feudal sway over a Druze and Christian population. And thus, the notable plan of the "Irlām," above alluded to, the appointment of Christian agents in every Druze village to be nominated by the patriarch, was simply a device, through that medium, to keep the Christians under his exclusive control, and to make them submissive to all his mandates. With such outposts thrown out in the very heart and centre of the Druze confederacy, he trusted that he might still uphold the long-enjoyed dictatorial power which he foresaw, under the new and altered circumstances, would otherwise elude his grasp, and for ever close the door against the intrusion of such doctrines as might emperil the working of that well organised ecclesiastical system which made every Christian within his flock his vassal and his slave. Most important is it to note and weigh this remarkable feature in the approaching crisis, for here we place the finger on the source of all those accumulated evils, which, with various accessories, and from different quarters, henceforth oppressed and desolated the Lebanon.

The elements of discord exercised by priestly ambition at length found vent. On the 14th September 1841, an affray took place between the Druzes and the Christians of Deir-el-Kamar, attended with the loss of five Christians and sixteen Druzes killed, and eight Christians and sixteen Druzes wounded. Some Christians of Deir-el-Kamar, crossing the deep ravine which separates it from the opposite Druze village of Bakleen, had trespassed on a shooting preserve near the latter place, belonging to their own feudal chief, Nasif Bey Abou Nakad, and shot down a partridge. The Druze watchers repulsed them, but merely using sticks. Far from acknowledging their error, the Christians sent word to Deir-el-Kamar, and were presently joined by a large reinforcement of their co-religionists armed to the teeth, who immediately commenced an indiscriminate firing on the Druzes.

The latter thus unprovokedly and brutally attacked, sprung to their arms and the mêlée soon became general. In the mean time the Christians of Deir-el-Kamar, seeing the battle engaged, from their heights, and also the various bodies of the Druzes who were rapidly approaching from every direction, were thrown into the wildest despair. The women ran about the streets tearing their hair and beating their breasts. The old men with firearms proceeded to the roofs of the houses to defend the town in case of an attack. The state of confusion soon became indescribable, and the dread of a general assault by the Druzes possessed all minds.

Fortunately for the Christian population, Colonel Rose, her Majesty's Consul-General, happened to be in the town at the time. With the utmost promptitude, and ordering a Druze sheik to accompany him, he galloped to the scene of conflict nearly two miles off, and gallantly threw himself between the combatants : his interference was effectual. Both parties listened to his reasoning and entreaties, and for this time, at least, the flames of civil war were extinguished ere they had time to gain head.

The attitude of defiance thus unequivocally assumed by the Christians, showed the Druzes that it was high time to concert measures for a general defence. Partial attacks upon them had occurred in other parts of the Lebanon. The Christians of Gezeen had wantonly killed three Druzes sent by the Jumblatts to collect their rents. The revengeful feelings of the Druzes had also been much excited by the loss of four of the principal sheiks of the house of Amad, killed at Baakleen, as well as some of their women, who had fallen in endeavouring to make peace. To crown all, the Maronite patriarch had openly declared, that if the Druzes persisted in demanding to be governed by a prince of their own sect, he and his clergy would head the Maronites, march against them and exterminate them.

The Emir Beshir, on his part, endeavoured to

deprive the Druze sheiks of their feudal privilege, and proceeded to levy a military force from amongst the Christians, their feudal dependents, thus directly invading the hereditary rights of the Abou Nakads. A general report also at this time gained ground, that the old Emir Beshir was about to be recalled and reinstated: a measure which the Druzes well knew, if accomplished, would pave the way to a return to their former state of weakness and disunion.

Under all these circumstances, it became a matter of life and death with them to strike a blow ere the means intended for their humiliation were completely matured. They had already entered into a compact with the Turks, and were, indeed, guided by their secret instructions.

On the morning of the 13th October the feudal array of the Jumblatts, the Abou Nakads, and the Amads, with their banners flying and kettle-drums beating, were seen, as if by enchantment, in possession of the various avenues leading to Deirel-Kamar, and crowning all the surrounding heights. Never was a combination more rapid or complete, or more characteristic of that secrecy, energy and activity, for which the Druzes are so remarkable in their military movements. The Christians, panic struck by the suddenness of the assault, snatched up their arms and ran about in the utmost consternation. The Druzes kept stealthily converging on the devoted town. For some hours they met with an irregular but vigorous resistance in the outskirts. These, however, they at last succeeded in taking possession of and burning. The Christians were finally driven back into the central square, where all their families began to congregate about sunset. Throughout the whole day the emir remained shut up in a small room carefully secured. Shortly after dark the principal suburbs were in a blaze. During the whole of the ensuing night, the town presented to view one grand but melancholy spectacle; the sky being lighted up with rolling volumes of flame, whilst every now and then might be heard the desponding cries of the Christians, the furious tolling of the Maronite bells, and the exulting yells of the Druzes.

The struggle continued without interruption

during the 14th and 15th, while other villages in the neighbourhood were at the same time successfully attacked by the Abou Nakads, with considerable slaughter of their Christian inhabitants. On the 16th, Colonel Rose, accompanied by Ayoub Pasha, arrived from Beyrout just in time to save Deir-el-Kamar from utter destruction, and its male population from a relentless massacre. Twenty Christian prisoners had already been put to the edge of the sword. When Druze vengeance is once aroused, it is remorseless. They imbrue their hands in blood with a savage joy that is incredible. Yet, as a general principle, they never touch women.

The war cry had now been sounded throughout the Lebanon. Both sects, throughout all their districts, rushed to arms. The Maronite patriarch, furious at the unexpected defeat at Deir-el-Kamar, loudly demanded to be carried in his bed, ill as he was, to the front of the Christian forces, "there to unfurl the standard of the Cross. and die at their head."

The Greek Catholic Bishop of Zach/é, issued a proclamation, calling on all true Christians to come forward without fear. "Strengthen," said he, "the arms of activity; never turn back after a victory, without destroying to the end; spare the females, but as to everything else, such as murdering, plundering, burning, be sure to do all this, and continue your prayers and confessions, for this is a holy war."

Wherever conflicts took place between the Druzes and Christians, the victory invariably rested with the former. The main object of the latter was to relieve the town of Deir-el-Kamar, but all their attempts were fruitless. The Christians of the Greek Church generally joined with the Druzes in attacking the Maronites. The Shehab emirs headed the Maronite reinforcements, hoping, if successful, to procure the restoration of the old Emir Beshir, and the reinstatement of their family in power. In less than ten days the Druzes had completely subdued the Maronites residing amongst them, sacking and burning their villages and convents.

They now prepared to carry the war into the purely Maronite districts, north of the Dog river. Fortunately for the Maronites, Naaman Bey Jumblatt, whose influence over his sect was paramount, now displayed the greatest moderation, wholly opposed such an onward movement, and even declared that if any Druze force crossed that river he should forthwith attack it. Sitting up night and day, surrounded by his secretaries, he wrote upwards of ten thousand letters to different influential Druzes and Christians, imploring them to cease from their fratricidal war. Thus was the triumphal course of the Druzes stopped by one of their own leaders. The Maronite patriarch, bewildered by the sweeping successes of those he had thought to exterminate, shut himself up at first in a room in his convent, and finally negotiated for refuge on a British man-of-war.

At Deir-el-Kamar, after three weeks close blockade, the Christians were summoned to surrender and give up their arms. On the 5th of October, the Emir Beshir, finding himself a helpless prisoner, determined to evacuate the town, agreeing to conditions drawn up by the Druzes and ratified by the Pasha of Beyrout. His exit was one continued scene of mortification. On leaving his palace, accompanied by some mounted attendants, his sword and dagger were taken from him with such violence as to wound his hands. He was deprived of his turban and the greatest part of his dress. One Druze levelled his piece at him, but it missed fire. On approaching Beyrout he saw his own private residence, the houses of the Shehaab emirs, and those of the inhabitants in the villages of Baabda and Haded all in flames. He beheld his Maronite subjects flying in the greatest disorder along the front of the Turkish camp of regular troops, who had been ostensibly sent out to restore order, but who all along remained tranquil and even rejoicing spectators of every kind of outrage. The Turkish irregular cavalry were charging, wounding, and robbing the unfortunate fugitives, even to stripping the very women of their clothes, which the Druzes in pity had spared them. So keenly was the infamous conduct of the Turkish troops felt, that the Maronites declared " they would sooner be plundered by the Druzes than protected by the Turks."

It now became clear that this first attempt of the Maronite patriarch and his colleagues to establish an exclusive ascendancy in the Lebanon, by weakening, if not destroying, the Druze element, had signally failed. The emptiness of their boastful taunts and denunciations were fully exposed. Their lofty and ill-judged schemes of aggrandisement had completely miscarried. The vials of wrath they had prepared for the Druzes had recoiled fearfully on their own heads. All the bitterness of their hearts had been fruitlessly exhaled, and nought was now left them of their venom but the sting.

To the Turks this boiling and fuming of the worst passions of human nature, surging over into the fury of civil strife and discord, was as the odour of a sweet smelling sacrifice. Wilfully and purposely did they promote the hateful struggle; for through such bloody dissensions they saw the only chance of establishing their own exclusive sway over the Lebanon. In the Christians of the Lebanon they saw a ready nucleus for the intrusion and the permanent preponderance of a foreign power, gradually enabling them to advance new pretensions, to acquire new rights, and finally, perhaps, to establish a quasi-independence, formidable and menacing to their own political existence.

Irrelative of their innate hatred of Christianity itself, the Turks perceive full well that of all the various races under their dominion, the Christian race alone gives signs of dangerous vitality; and for this reason they watch, with lynx-eyed vigilance, every quarter of their empire where it threatens, under more than ordinarily propitious circumstances, to raise its odious front. Were the Christian element to become strong, consolidated, and flourishing in the Lebanon,— which, however, it can only be under the constant supervision and effectual protection of the European states,— the position of the Turks, as a dominant and monopolising power, throughout Syria itself, would be materially affected, and the various adjacent tribes might gradually emerge from centuries of moral prostration.

Thus the main, it may be said, the sole object which the Turks have had in view for the last few years in the Lebanon, is, at whatever risk and by any means however reckless or nefarious, to keep down an element which presents itself with such dangerous concomitants, and to cut out, as it were, if necessary (alas! the metaphor is too sadly significant), a cancer which, in their eyes, threatens to eat into their very vitals. This is the key to their entire policy; and, bearing this in mind, their whole subsequent action, however otherwise incredible and repugnant to all feelings of morality, becomes perfectly consistent and perspicuous.

The Christian governor of the Lebanon had been forcibly ejected, and the Turks had gained a temporary triumph. For the purpose of acquiring and retaining an exclusive influence in the mountain, they had excited the Druzes against the Christians, and encouraged the former in their desire to be independent of the latter. So perfectly cognisant were they of all the movements of the Druzes, that the Seraskier made the remarkable declaration, that "he knew the Druzes intended to attack Deir-el-Kamar fourteen days before the event occurred." *

Notwithstanding the constant and repeated advice and remonstrances of the European consuls, the Turkish authorities never took the slight-

* Syrian Correspondence, Part II. p. 897.

est measure to check hostilities, or to punish those who were the first to cause a collision. Regrets were profusely expressed, ample promises made; troops were even ordered out to certain positions, but the latter never in any one instance made the least effort to prevent one party from attacking the other. Whole villages were burnt to the ground under their very eyes. Nay, more; as if in open mockery of his professions of neutrality, the general excuse urged for his criminal collusion, the Seraskier actually sent five camel-loads of ammunition to the head-quarters of the Maronite forces; and having thus supplied them with the means of carrying on the war, the next day, to save appearances, sent them an order to make peace with their adversaries, on pain of suffering the severest penalties. The Druzes at the same time received ample supplies of ammunition from the same quarter.

If such was the procedure of the Turks in the pashalick of Beyrout, even more indecent and outrageous was it in that of Damascus. There Najib Pasha, the worst possible specimen of the corrupt and blood-thirsty race of Turkish fanatics, had, ever since his arrival, been strenuously exciting and reviving the old Mohammedan antipathies.

In his relations with the anti-Lebanon, which was within his jurisdiction, he scarcely even deigned to assume a mask. Although the Christians of that district, mostly belonging to the Greek Church, had not the remotest connection with the Maronites of the Lebanon, nor had ever shown any disposition whatever to disturb the peace, he at once proceeded to make them feel the full weight of a deliberate persecution. Seizing, degrading, and imprisoning the Emir Saadàdeen Shehab, the Mohammedan governor of Harbuju, their capital, whose sole crime was his moderation and his consequent popularity, he replaced him by the celebrated Druze chief, Shibli-el-Arrian, who had so long headed the Druze insurrection against Ibrahim Pasha.

The first acts of this functionary, according to his secret instructions, was to disarm the Christians, in direct violation of the guarantee given to the Syrians by the Porte, at the hands of the British government; to seize and imprison their most influential men, and to distribute large supplies of powder to the Druzes.

After some preliminary arrangements, he proceeded, at the head of 500 Turkish cavalry, and some thousands of his Druzes, commanded by their sheiks, to march upon and attack the town of Zach*l*é, situated at the foot of one of the eastern slopes of the Lebanon, and overlooking the fertile valley of the Bekaa, the ancient Cœlo-Syria. On his way thither, he wantonly plundered and burnt several harmless Christian villages. Said Bey Jumblatt made himself conspicuous in this raid, by attacking the village of Sagbeen, and indiscriminately massacring 210 men, women, and children.*

Again, on hearing of these occurrences, the European consuls, stepped forward in a body, to endeavour by impassioned remonstrance, to avert the terrible fate which was evidently impending over all the Christian sects of the Lebanon, without distinction, and probably, as the storm rolled on, over the entire Christian population of Syria. They were met as usual by expressions of af-

* Syrian Correspondence, Part I. p. 149.

fected ignorance or assumed astonishment. At last it became so palpable that the Turks were doggedly bent on crushing and trampling out every remaining vestige of strength which might still exist in the Christian ranks, that they felt their position as remonstrants becoming "absolutely ludicrous."* Ludicrous! nay, rather humiliating and degrading; that the representatives of the five great Christian powers of Europe should have been authorised and commissioned by their sovereigns to interpose between the Turks and their bleeding victims, should have been reduced to the attitude of supplicants, and then forced to stand by helpless spectators of one persistent and gigantic outrage against their common faith.

All, in fact, felt and declared, that they were vainly struggling against a preconcerted plan, emanating from Constantinople itself; and that the Sultan's authorities in Syria would never have acted as they were doing, unless they had been authorised to do so by secret instructions from the Porte.† A conclusion amply warranted by

* Syrian Correspondence, Part II. p. 116.   † Ibid.

an intercepted letter from Najib Pasha to the Seraskier, in which the latter is directed "not to trouble himself in the least about what is going on in the Lebanon, inasmuch as everything that had taken place there had been done with the full sanction of the Porte."*

The Druze attack upon Zachlé fortunately proved abortive, otherwise the Christians there would inevitably have experienced the effects of Druze ferocity and Turkish treachery. For Reshid Pasha, ostensibly ordered thither to prevent the conflict, purposely delayed his movement in order to give the Druzes time to advance, while his aide-de-camp who preceded him, after having called on the Christians to give up their arms, promising them complete protection, absolutely went over to the camp of the Druzes, and accompanied them the following day in their unsuccessful onslaught.

The immediate consequence of the triumphs of the Druzes, thus encouraged and supported by the Turks, was a widespread outburst of Mohammedan fanaticism against the Christians

* Syrian Correspondence, Part II. p. 283.

all over Syria. In the great towns a general rising was daily expected. Native Christians, and even Europeans, were insulted, beaten, and knocked down in the bazaars. British men-of-war were stationed off the sea-coast towns, to reassure their trembling inhabitants. Whole families hourly thronged the beach, who had fled from the interior in terror and dismay. In several of the villages about Damascus, the Turks burnt the churches to the ground, threatening to kill the men and carry the women and children into slavery. In Damascus itself, the Mohammedans, emboldened by the impunity of such proceedings, loudly demanded the destruction of the churches which had been erected without the Sultan's firman during the Egyptian occupation. They boasted that the time had come for binding the rayahs to the exact fulfilment of all the articles contained in the famous contract of Omar-ibn-il-Hotab. A petition was got up for the removal of all European agents. Finally, instigated by the secret approval of Najib Pasha, they talked publicly of a general massacre of the Christians.

In the midst of the general consternation which had seized on the Christian community, it was ascertained that the pasha was making preparations to leave the city, under pretence of accompanying the Mecca pilgrimage, as far as the Houran. Mr. Wood, her Majesty's consul, at once saw that this was merely a pretext on his part to escape the responsibility of whatever horrors might occur during his absence. First addressing himself to some of the principal ulemas, he, simply by the weight of his personal influence, brought them to the point of using their endeavours to allay the religious ferment which was hourly augmenting. Then, going to the pasha, he expostulated with him, warned him as to the grave and awful consequences which must inevitably result to the empire itself, should he persist in his present conduct, and implored him to remain at his post. The hoary fanatic was abashed. Awaking as from a stupor, he issued orders for assuring the public tranquillity,—and the bloody wave was stayed.

CHAP. III.

Peace.— Omar Pasha Governor of the Lebanon, January 1842.— Mustapha Pasha. — The Maronite Emir Beshir Ahmad Abou Lamā.—Omar Pasha seizes five Druze Chiefs. — Druze Revolt. — Shibli-el-Arrian. — January 1, 1843, Omar Pasha defeats the Druzes. — Emir Ahmad Raslan and Emir Haider Abou Lamā the Druze and Christian Kaimmakams. — January 1845, Said Bey Jumblatt and Said Bey. — In April, Maronite Attack on the Druzes. — Defeat of the Christians.

THROUGHOUT the Lebanon the fires of civil war gradually burnt out. Thus ended a contest, induced in the first instance by the grasping ambition and bigoted intolerance of the Maronite patriarch; engaged in by the Druzes with all the desperation of a people struggling for their nationality; and lashed into fury by the Turks, ever startling with convulsive clutch at the slightest throb or pulsation of the Christian heart.

Its immediate results exhibited a loss of more than three thousand lives, and destruction of property to the amount of nearly half a million of pounds. But even more deplorable was it, as leaving in the breasts of the hostile factions such seeds of animosity, as might at any future time be stimulated into fatal activity, to work out the policy of their common masters. The Christians in vain sought for indemnification at all adequate to their losses. The Turkish authorities cared not to press upon the Druzes for restoration of plunder, in which they themselves had so largely shared; and though they talked with seeming earnestness before the European consuls, of the necessity of reimbursement, and even of retribution, they were far too cunning to institute any effective measures against a sect which had rendered them such signal services.

The Emir Beshir Kassim was ignominiously degraded from his office, and sent a prisoner to Constantinople, and on the 15th January, 1842, Omar Pasha was appointed governor of the Lebanon. About the same time Mustapha arrived at Beyrout, as extraordinary commissioner from the Porte, to inquire into the causes of the late outbreak, and to devise measures for the restoration of order. A more unhappy choice could not possibly have been made. It soon appeared that his sole object was to inflame still farther the unhappy dissensions which already existed, and to excite the feelings of the Mohammedan sects in such a manner as to increase with tenfold energy their ordinary antipathy to the Christians.

It is certain that he thus acted in conformity with his secret instructions. The Porte had at this moment a point of vital importance to its own interests to carry, and it only selected him as a fitting instrument. In order to carry this point, it was essential that the Christians themselves should be made to appear desirous of being ruled by a Turk. This was the mission of Mustapha Pasha. Accordingly, the Christians were told that they were at full liberty to express their wishes, by way of petition, as to whom they would wish to be the governor of the Lebanon. The Druzes were summoned to exercise the same privilege. The right thus conferred, in a manner so apparently magnanimous, was now to be counteracted and circumvented, so as to render it subservient to the furtherance of Turkish policy.

Whether by bribery and corruption, or by threats and intimidation, the voice of public opinion was to be unscrupulously stifled.

Had the Christians, and even the Druzes, been left really unfettered in their choice, there cannot be a doubt that the Shehabs would have been restored to power; for several of the Druze sheiks, ancient partisans of the old Emir Beshir, would have voted in their favour. Turkish agents were forthwith sent amongst the people, to prevent, if possible, the realisation of such views. Such was the venality and pusillanimity of the Christian aristocracy, that numbers were gained over by the most ordinary presents, such as pelisses or shawls, combined with promises of further favour and preferment, to abandon their best interests, and, utterly regardless of past experience or future consequences, to vote for the permanent supremacy over them, of those very beings who had but one short month before been revelling in their blood and trampling on their religion.

The Maronite Emir Beshir Ahmad Abou Lamā, now for the first time gained over to the Turks by a large grant of land and a round sum of money, began to play the part of a Turkish tool, which some years afterwards it was his lot to enact in a more extensive sphere, and with consequences proportionably fatal to the welfare of his sect.

Where bribery failed to work its way, threats and blows, and every species of personal indignity were dealt out to and heaped upon the unhappy Christians, to compel them to vote for a Turkish governor. Several died from the effects of the barbarous bastinado to which they were subjected. A corps of two thousand Albanians, the most ill-disciplined, lawless and ferocious ruffians that were ever drawn together, had lately landed at Beyrout. It was whispered through the mountain that these pests were to be quartered in the Christian villages. The Maronites began to tremble for the sanctity of their homes, and already pictured to themselves their wives violated, their children torn away, their property plundered. The panic soon became general, and hundreds put their trembling hands to petitions imploring the Sultan, in his great kindness and consideration, to allow them to be governed by a Turkish Pasha! Such the proceedings, such the mercies of the Turks.

Though the dismissal of the Emir Beshir Kassim was fully justifiable, from his general unfitness to hold the arduous and responsible post to which he had been elevated, yet there cannot be a doubt that the coarse and brutal treatment to which he was subsequently exposed, and his hasty deportation, were intended as visitations for the unpardonable offence of having procured his appointment through the interest, and on the recommendation, of the British government, and of having looked to that government for support and protection. Mustapha Pasha, indeed, made no hesitation in openly expressing his belief, that so long as a Christian ruled in the Lebanon, he must look more or less to a foreign power; and that foreign agents would find the means of interfering in its affairs, not only to the prejudice of the Porte, but of the inhabitants themselves.* The which simply means, that were the Lebanon under well regulated and well defined Christian

* Syrian Correspondence, Part II. p. 202.

administration, the Turks could not, at their good will and pleasure, crush it under their iron heels.

Most remarkable indeed is it, but not the less painfully true, that although the Turks owed their restoration to power in Syria, entirely and exclusively to the exertions of the Christian powers, a circumstance which in ordinary breasts would have excited some feelings of grateful recognition, yet no sooner were they installed, than all their exertions were directed towards beating down every species of European influence throughout the country, and particularly in the Lebanon; towards intimidating all the native chiefs from having any relations with European agents, recalling all the promises which had been formally given, and annulling all the privileges and concessions which had been granted to the Lebanites, through their solemn intervention.

The better to carry out their designs in this respect, it is a common artifice with them, from time to time, to circulate rumours of a threatened invasion of their territories by some Christian power, and to hint at the necessity of a levy " en masse" of all true followers of the Prophet, to resist the inroads of the infidel. While they thus sow broadcast the seeds of fanatical hatred of everything Christian amongst the lower orders of the Mussulman population, they ingratiate themselves by acts of extraordinary condescension with the ulemas and sheiks of religion, imbue them with feelings of contempt for the Franks, and allure such as may momentarily stray beyond the orbit of their influence, with hopes of patronage and reward; inexorably crushing all who are countenanced and favoured by Europeans, and ostentatiously upholding all who are opposed to them.

Knowing that the English will be the last to desert them, they take a cowardly pleasure in selecting English consuls as objects of their slights, and in purposely neglecting the vindication and support of English interests, in order to show triumphantly that they are perfectly independent of all foreign control. By such devices they rally the confidence of the Mussulman population, and embolden them in the display of a haughty, overbearing, and menacing behaviour towards the rayahs. This is the unchangeable and inherent policy of the Turks; the only one, whatever other garb of policy political expediency may induce them to assume, which they will ever pursue, for, in their incorrigible blindness, they consider it essential to the predominance of their race.*

Consequently, it may be accepted with all the sequential certainty of an axiom and its corollary, that whenever they make any promises to the European powers, or bind themselves by any engagements, to ameliorate the condition of the Christians throughout their empire, they immediately set to work a secret counter-current, exciting the religious passions of their co-religionists in such a manner as shall render the performance of those promises, or the execution of such engagements, absolutely impossible, except at the risk of such an outbreak of Mohammedan fanaticism, as will endanger the lives and properties of the very class they profess to elevate and improve. To use their own remarkable avowal,

* Syrian Correspondence, Part II. p. 216.

"the Turks cannot regain their lost position and influence without they return to fanaticism."*

Omar Pasha soon found his position at Deir-el-Kamar surrounded with difficulties. The Druze sheiks, elated with their conquests, affected an air of independence, asserted their feudal superiority over the Christians, and denied the right of any to intervene between them. In many instances they proceeded to ill-treat and abuse such of the Christians as were peculiarly obnoxious to them; and when the former presented petitions to the Pasha, asking for protection and redress, they resented it as an insult. "What," said they, "we have fought for the Turks and conquered; we gave them enormous bribes; we gave them a large share of the spoil, and are we now to be coerced by the power which we have created?"†

They further declared, that, "if any attempts were made to oblige them to act differently towards the Christians, and to give up the property and lands which they had taken from them, they

---

* Syrian Correspondence, Part II. p. 173.
† Ibid. Part II. pp. 209, 210.

would at once expose the secret connection which had all along existed between them and the Turks."

So menacing became the Druze dictation, that Omar Pasha felt a reinforcement of troops absolutely necessary for the vindication of his authority. The Seraskier refused his application to that effect, with a taunting reply, that he was an infidel and a traitor for thus breaking with the Druzes. Later instructions, however, directed him to take immediate measures for arresting a movement which was clearly verging on open rebellion. Accordingly, on the 6th April, he asked five of the leading chiefs to dinner, and after the repast was over, suddenly had them surrounded and made prisoners. The same night he hurried them off under escort to Sidon. This act of combined treachery and vigour was intended to effect two objects: — to show the European powers that Turkish rule could make itself feared and respected, and to strike a salutary terror into the mountain aristocracy, both Druze and Christian, now especially appealed to by the Turkish authorities, to support their views of bringing the Lebanon under their exclusive dominion.

Notwithstanding a strong effervescence of feeling amongst the Druzes, on the seizure of their chiefs, they were not in a condition as yet to attempt an attack on Omar Pasha's garrison at Beit-ed-Deen, near Deir-el-Kamar. Several Maronite leaders had offered their services to the Turks, in case they were menaced by the Druzes; and for the latter to defend themselves against such a combination would have been clearly impossible.

The Turks now, with their usual wiliness, and also with their usual success, divided the Druzes into two parties; and, after throwing the above-mentioned chiefs into the prison at Beyrout, took others into their pay and favour. Having thus, for the moment, neutralised Druze hostility, they spared no means and stopped at no alternatives to force a general expression of the popular voice in their favour. Agents were sent throughout the mountain with petitions, for a Turkish governor, ready drawn out, which, by entreaties, promises and threats, they got numbers to sign. Many were tortured into compliance. There was one influential Christian chief, however, who boldly confronted them, and had rallied a considerable party to his views. It was in recklessly pursuing this malcontent that they roused a spirit amongst the Maronites which involved them in fresh complications. The troops they sent to seize him in the fastnesses of Bisherry were suddenly attacked by the mountaineers, and ignominiously defeated with great loss of life.

The Druzes saw their opportunity, and immediately entered into negotiations with the Maronites to effect a common rising against the Government. Had the most ordinary principle of patriotism presided over these attempts at reconciliation, the better to overwhelm a common foe, the power of the Turks might have been seriously compromised. But mutual jealousy and distrust rendered all the endeavours of both parties abortive. The Druzes promised to declare in favour of the Shehabs, but on condition that the Maronites should first begin the insurrectionary movement. The Christians stipulated that the Druzes should strike the first blow, and give a written document, signed with the seals of all their leading sheiks, demanding a Shehab, as a guarantee for their good faith, and one which might be shown to the Turks in case of their deserting or betraying them. Hence arose a sort of dispute which could never be settled, both sides suspecting each other's intentions.

The Turks, in the mean time, were fully alive to the necessity of thwarting this ominous alliance, and lost no time in bringing all their allurements to bear upon the well-known and often experienced venality of the Maronites. A vizierial order — giving protection to the Maronite patriarch, the liberation of such of their chiefs as had been thrown into prison on account of their refusing to petition for a Turkish governor, the promise of restoration of the property plundered by the Druzes, a sword to one, a shawl to another, a watch and a few hundred piastres to a third,— sufficed to soothe the Maronite disaffection, and to break up the threatened coalition.

Such is the way in which the Turks ever maintained their power. Not by vindicating their authority, as a legitimate government ought to do, but by exciting and playing upon the worst passions of human nature; by setting sect against sect; subdividing again, by corruption and intrigue, these sects amongst themselves; by bribing the worthless to betray their relations, their religion, and their country; and by dissolving all the ties which create confidence and happiness amongst mankind.

In this manner they contrived, for a few months, to ward off the conspiracies which menaced their already precarious position. The patience of the Druzes, however, had its limits; and they determined at length to throw down the gauntlet of defiance to the Turks, even though they stood alone. Their famous chief, Shibli-el-Arrian, now appeared as their leader. Under his direction, towards the end of November 1842, thousands of them marched upon Beit-ed-Deen, occupied all the adjacent heights, cut off the supplies of water, and blockaded the Turkish garrison with Omar Pasha at their head. Having successfully resisted a sortie made by the latter, the Druzes grew emboldened in their demands. They insisted on the liberation of their sheiks, the immediate dismissal of Omar Pasha, and exemption from conscription or disarmament.

In the negotiations which ensued, they were told by the Turkish authorities that the cause of all the late proceedings against them was their not having paid the indemnities loudly demanded by the Christians; an artful plea, meant to transfer from themselves the unpopularity of the demand. Shibli-el-Arrian not only parried but turned the blow on the Turks. He boldly stated that the Turks ought alone to pay these indemnities, because they had last year, by promises of reward and plunder, incited the Druzes to fall on the Christians, and because the Druzes had actually expended 300,000*l.* in bribes to the functionaries of the Porte in Syria, including the Grand Vizier at Constantinople himself.

The Turks now determined to make a final effort to vindicate their authority thus openly insulted, and, fortunately for them, the movement they made was effectual.

A body of Turks and Albanians, with some pieces of artillery, marching up towards Deir-el-Kamar from Sidon, took the Druze forces in the rear, while Omar Pasha, with his garrison and a large body of Maronite cavalry, headed by their chiefs, operated simultaneously in their front. The Druzes, after a brave and protracted resistance of some hours, gave way, and dispersed in various directions. Their leading sheiks fled into the Houran, while Shibli-el-Arrian, dispirited at this sudden and unexpected reverse of fortune, made his submission to the Pasha of Damascus, not without strong suspicions, however, of having been bribed to betray his countrymen and desert their cause.

Alarmed at tidings which reached it on all sides of the utter disorganisation which existed in the Lebanon, and unprepared to contend with what seemed daily to be assuming the proportions of a general rebellion, the Porte found itself necessarily compelled to yield to circumstances, abandoned for the moment its favourite object, and settled that each of the two sects should have a governor of its own creed and nation. On the 1st of January, 1843, the Emir Haider Abou Lamā and the Emir Achmed Raslan were invested as kaimmakams, respectively, for the Christians and the Druzes.

This apparently equitable and satisfactory solution of a much vexed question, however, only gave rise to greater difficulties and fresh complications. Had the whole Christian population resided together in one part of the mountain, and the entire Druze population in another, within prescribed boundaries, the plan would have been as practicable as it was simple. But thousands of Christians, both Greek and Maronite, lived in the Druze districts, as feudal dependents of the Druze sheiks, who exercised a right over them inherited from father to son, for ages. The direct rule of the Christian governor over the Christians, implying his absolute authority over them wherever they might reside, at once abolished this right, and struck at the root of those privileges which the Druzes regarded as the mainstay of their power. In fact, it was the attempt of the Maronite patriarch to effect such an important change, in the preceding year, which was the cause of the civil war.

The Maronites, on the contrary, who lived amongst the Druzes hailed the change as a signal of delivery from what they called Druze bondage.

Hence an immediate source of renewed jealousies, heart-burnings and animosities between the two sects. Nevertheless, it is remarkable that the Greek Christians unanimously refused to accept the proffered boon, and declared their preference for Druze rule over them; thus belying the constantly repeated assertion of the Maronites, that the Christians could never be happy under the Druzes, and that death would be preferable to submitting to their intolerable tyranny. The fact was, the Greek Christians found a refuge in the bosom of the Druze chiefs from the fierce bigotry and persecution of the Maronite patriarch, who, ever since the Shehabs had embraced the Roman Catholic faith, had invariably made the ruling member of that family an instrument in his hands for furthering and promoting his views of religious ascendancy over the whole of the Lebanon.

The newly appointed Christian kaimmakam, though not a Shehab, was a zealous Maronite, and would inevitably succumb to the same influence. This the Greek Christians well knew, and they dreaded a renewal of Maronite patriarchal dictation, under which their civil and ecclesiastical rights had been not only disregarded but unscrupulously set aside. Their convents had been deprived of their lands on plausible pretexts. Proselytism had been carried on by the unworthy means of intimidation and abstraction of property, which was only restored when the truth of Catholicism had been acknowledged. If Maronite authority could thus treat Christians, is it strange that it should have sat heavily on the Druzes? This preference on the part of the Greek Christians is a most important and instructive fact. It proves that Druze resistance, and even violence, was not so much directed against Christianity as against Maronite ambition and presumption, and the domineering views of an intolerant priesthood.

Week after week and month after month passed away in vain endeavours to find a common ground on which the two sects might merge their differences. Neither would resign their rights nor their pretensions. The Druzes, with natural and excusable pertinacity, refused to accept an arrangement which they clearly foresaw would ultimately reduce them, as a political body, to absolute impotence and insignificance. The Maronites, excited by their clergy, talked loudly of the intolerable yoke of Druze oppression, and declared their determination never to submit to it again.

Negotiations, conferences in presence of the Turkish authorities, assurances of supervision and protection from the European powers, proposals and counter-proposals, propositions such as that the Maronites living amongst the Druzes should have every facility given them to emigrate; or that they should be allowed to appoint agents of their own to represent them, and look after their interests, with the Druze jurisdiction,—all was in vain. At length, the Maronite patriarch, mad with vexation and disappointment, again fulminated the thunders of his wrath. "Maronite or Druze supremacy," he declared, "the blow must be struck, and he who strikes first will have two chances to one in his favour," a dictum, which, though he was the first to enounce it as a theory, he invariably found to his cost the Druzes best knew how to reduce to practice.

The elements of disorder thus rife soon broke out afresh. The Maronites had first, as before, sounded the note of defiance. Assassinations and their necessary reprisals soon gave tokens of the coming storm. The ordinary avocations of industrial labour were now abandoned. Both parties issued their proclamations, and distributed their outposts, like two opposing armies entering into a campaign.

The Turks again adopted their unalterable policy, delighted at the prospect of renewed miseries to the Christians, and already in imagination carving out a path over their lifeless bodies and ruined tenements to the attainment of their corrupt and selfish views. Ever busy in the work of underhand intrigue, they warned the Druzes against yielding one iota to the contemptuous demands of Christian insolence; while, at the same time, so far from preventing hostilities, they absolutely encouraged the Maronites to attack the Druzes, openly telling them they had their leave to do so.

Full scope being thus given to their movements, the Maronites no longer made any secrets of their designs. The Shehabs openly declared that an appeal to the sword was a matter unchangeably determined in their counsels, and sealed with the signet of desperation. The Maronites in the mixed districts exclaimed, "We cannot exist with the Druzes, either they or we must be destroyed or leave the country," while their hostile preparations, their military organisation with military names, together with the incessant purchase of arms and ammunition, embittered still more the feelings of the Druzes, already exasperated by the former attempts made on their independence.

The self-constituted municipal body of Maronites at Deir-el-Kamar gave the strictest orders to all their co-religionists, on pain of death, not to enter into friendly or indeed into any intercourse whatever with the rival sect. And they made good their injunctions. An unfortunate Maronite priest was put to death by their orders because he had entered into relations with the Druze sheik, Said Bey Jumblatt. The lives of others who disobeyed their orders were attempted, while many were wounded and beaten. Such efficacious means produced the desired result. In a short time, Christian tenants dared not, however much they secretly wished it, go near their Druze landlords. In some places they refused to pay them their rents. To speak to a Druze became a misdemeanour, to associate with him was punished as a treason.

Large funds had been received by the Maronite patriarch, from France and Austria, for the purpose of relieving the terrible distress endured by the Christians in consequence of the last civil war. He at once appropriated them to the promotion of a second; authorising his clergy to pay the combatants four piastres a day to each man, and to purchase arms and ammunition wherever they could be obtained. Knowing that the great body of the Maronites would not engage in a war, simply to destroy the political rights of the Druzes, the justice of which, indeed, the more dispassionate amongst them were ever ready to admit, he made of a war of party a war of religion. The Druzes, the enemies of the cross, the infidels, were to be exterminated or driven out of the land.

There cannot be a doubt that it was the hope of the Maronite clergy, by awakening a deep feeling of hatred and religious enthusiasm amongst their followers, to enable the Christian population to overwhelm the counterpoise to their power and influence in the Lebanon, which the Druze element prevented; and it is not improbable that, had they succeeded in this project, they would then have turned their thoughts towards freeing Christianity from another trammel — Ottoman rule.*

A grand meeting of all the principal Druze sheiks, — convened at Mucktara, the seat of Said Bey Jumblatt, about the end of January 1845, — demonstrated that the Druzes were in movement. Although the Druzes are in ordinary times divided into two great parties, inspired by sentiments of mutual jealousy, yet in times of civil commotion, the grand centre of combination, of council, and of action, is the family of Jumblatt. During the first years of the present century, its then head and chief, Sheik Beshir Jumblatt, was the virtual ruler of the Lebanon. His immense wealth, his extensive territories, and his numerous partisans and adherents, not only in his own sect but amongst the Maronites themselves, made his influence all powerful.

For a long time he shared equally with the

* Syrian Correspondence, Part II. p. 161.

Emir Beshir Shehab all the functions of government; but when he perceived, at last, that the latter was bent on elevating the Christian population to a position which threatened to endanger the long-enjoyed supremacy of the Druzes; he broke out against him in open revolt. Though bringing into the field a vastly superior numerical force, and joined even by several Maronite chiefs with their followers, he failed in his attempt, principally owing to the action of some Turkish troops which the Emir Beshir had obtained from the famous Djezzar, then Pasha of Acre. Escaping from the field of battle, the Sheik Beshir was afterwards seized and taken a prisoner to Acre, where Djezzar put him to death.

His three sons, then mere children, remained in exile during the remainder of the Emir Beshir's administration, but returned to find their ancestral home at Muchtara in ruins, on the restoration of the Sultan's government in 1840. The eldest, Naaman Bey, retired into strictly private life shortly after the civil war of 1841. The youngest, Ismail, was sent for his education to England, but, after only a year's absence, returned with his mind completely disordered, and lingering a few years in hopeless lunacy, died. The name, the fortune, and the prestige of the Jumblatts had now to be sustained by Said Bey alone.

Young and energetic, the Bey had already, during the late war, given proofs of bravery, and displayed the lurkings of a sanguinary ferocity, — qualities whch strongly recommended him to the daring and savage nature of the Druzes. He had early secured the patronage, and even the official protection, of the British government, which imagined it saw, in the effective maintenance of his power and ascendancy, a means of establishing throughout the Druze sect a political influence, to counterbalance that possessed by France over the Maronites. For two whole months the incessant arrival and departure of messengers, the secret conferences by day and night, and the extraordinary drains upon his hospitality, evinced that Said Bey's divan was in full and constant activity.

The Maronites, on their parts, held their assemblies, issued their mandates, and, by pompous proclamations, encouraged the Christians to stand ready for the hour of trial. The Shehab emirs came prominently forth as leaders. They formed a rallying point at Abeih, whither all the Christians in the mixed districts were summoned to gather. They were determined to fight, and to risk all hazards, for the restoration of the old Emir Beshir as sole governor of the mountain. The Maronite clergy preached the holy war in their churches, and led on their flocks in person to the various places of rendezvous.

The Druzes, according to their usual tactics or rather directions, pretended to be greatly alarmed by all these hostile proceedings, and implored Turkish interference to prevent the awful calamities of war. European consuls even eagerly seconded these laudable and praiseworthy sentiments, and pressed the departure of Turkish troops to the different scenes of threatened collision. The Turks only waited for the pretext to get on the scene; and with every expression of sincere desire to stop the effusion of blood, by their active intervention, and by the resolute exercise of their authority, at once proceeded to place their forces in such positions, and with such instructions, as might enable them most efficaciously to give aid and support to the Druzes, and to crush the Christians, on whom, in more than one instance, they deliberately fired.

In the month of April 1845, the long gathering storm burst, by a general attack, from the Maronites on all the Druze quarters. In the district of the Shoof, they were led on by their bishop, crucifix in hand, after having obtained the sanction of the Turkish officer stationed there for the assault. At the first onset they carried everything before them, burning and destroying fourteen Druze villages, and advancing to the very walls of Muchtara. Here, the contemplated scene of their crowning conquest, they unexpectedly encountered a crushing defeat, for a Turkish regiment, drawn up in front of Said Bey's palace, received them with a rolling fire of musketry, and stopped their presumptuous career.

At Abeih, after a fierce encounter, the Christians, under the Shehab emirs, were totally routed, and the latter closely blockaded by the Druzes in their castle; the Turkish troops looking on as quiet spectators of the conflict. The former finally surrendered themselves as prisoners, and were conducted by Colonel Rose in person to Beyrout. In all other parts of the Lebanon similar engagements occurred with similar results, the Turks wherever they appeared acting as the Druze reserve. And then came the old story of villages in flames, property destroyed, and Christian fugitives pursued by Druzes and Turkish irregulars, plundered, mutilated and slain. Hopes of Maronite ascendancy scattered to the winds, and Christianity itself, betrayed, insulted and abased.

Again the genius of diplomacy was taxed at Constantinople to find a conductor that might draw off the devastating elements of the periodical tornado of Turkish intrigue and treachery, Maronite priestly ambition, and Druze vindictiveness. Chekib Effendi was sent on a special mission to Syria towards the close of 1845, and after long inquiry and numerous deliberations, the government of the Lebanon was settled on what it was thought would prove a permanent basis.

The principle of two kaimmakams was confirmed,

each with his separate tribunal, at which the different sects had their representatives. A geographical boundary separated the two sects. The feudal rights of the Druzes over the Christians residing amongst them, were sanctioned and admitted, the latter appointing agents with each ruling Druze chief, to guard over their interests. The Turkish authorities would only act in the mountain, through the medium of the kaimmakams, whose forces alone were to be called into requisition, to recover dues or to maintain order.

The Christians of Deir-el-Kamar, in despair at the prospect of finding themselves, even though nominally represented by an agent, under the odious and tyrannical yoke of the Druze sheik, Abou Nakad, and secretly urged to the step by the Turks, prayed and petitioned for a Turkish governor. The boon was granted; but the insult offered to those Druzes sunk deep into their hearts. They never forgave it or forgot it. For years they lived within sight of, but exiled from that, their ancestral appanage. They saw it grow up and prosper, till it became a wealthy, flourishing Christian community. But within its precincts there were no revenues as of old, no feudal state, for them. They never passed it without gnashing their teeth. But they bided their time.

CHAP. IV.

Survey, 1856.— Said Bey Jumblatt. — Deir-el-Kamar and Zach*l*é, prosperous Christian Towns in Druze Districts. — Hasbeya, large Christian Village in the Anti-Lebanon. — Druze Tyranny and Fraud encouraged by the Turks.— French Interference causes a Mohammedan ferment. — Emir Beshir Abou Lamā, the Christian Kaimmakam.—Intolerance of the Maronite Patriarch; he instigates (1858-59) the Peasants to revolt against their Sheiks.

THE Turks accepted the new system with sullen consent and ill-concealed antipathy. They had gained nothing: their active intrigue and criminal collusion had alike failed in achieving their object, and the Lebanon was as far from them as ever.

In place of following the various incidents of greater or less importance, which mark the history of the Druzes and Maronites for the next few years, incidents which can have no interest beyond their immediate locality, we will at once take our stand in the year 1856, and from thence take a general survey of the social and political position occupied by both sects.

The Christian kaimmakam, honest in intention, and just in his proceedings, had given general satisfaction to his co-religionists and the Christians of other sects living within his jurisdiction, until his death in 1854. But the Turks had not left him alone. Putting forward secretly their well tried and successful tool, the Emir Beshir Abou Lamā, they contrived, through his agency, to throw the Maronite districts into considerable confusion about the year 1851. The settled tranquillity and growing prosperity of the Christians was grating to their feelings, as affording evidence that the constitution, as it was called, of Chekib Effendi was working well. The emissaries of this emir were consequently found getting up agitation, signing petitions against the kaimmakam, and even exhibiting a display of force, by stopping the roads and resisting the local functionaries. The latter, of course, applied in vain to the Turkish authorities to take measures for checking a spirit so impeding to his administration, and his power and authority at last became seriously menaced.

Fortunately for the peace of the Lebanon England had an ambassador at that time at

Constantinople, in Lord Stratford de Redcliffe, who kept a watchful eye on its welfare, and who knew, at the same time, how to make the Turks respect him and obey him. By his usual prompt, energetic and salutary interference, their wiles were baffled, their designs exposed, and their action forced into a right direction. A very short time after his potent voice had made itself heard in the Turkish councils, the movement against the kaimmakam died a natural death.

The Druzes, partly by their own valour, but principally owing to the moral and physical support which they had received from the Turks, had succeeded in vindicating their rights and defeating the Maronite aggression. Their nationality had been admitted and preserved. Their feudal privilege, even over the Christians, sanctioned. Never had they enjoyed a pre-eminence so advantageous and promising. But the events of the last few years, the constant struggle for self-preservation with the Christians, in which they had been engaged, and the triumph with which they had emerged from the contest, had not unnaturally embittered their feelings of sectarian hatred, and engendered notions in their breasts of a haughty and vindictive superiority.

And thus it was, that as time rolled on, their treatment of the Christians under their immediate jurisdiction became more and more oppressive. The agents who were nominally placed near the Druze chiefs to act as joint arbitrators with them, in case of dispute or of complaint between Druzes and Christians, soon found themselves reduced to nonentity, and compelled to stand by, silent and helpless spectators of wrong and injustice. To such an extent did the domineering tyranny of some of the sheiks proceed, that it became usual with them, as their fancy dictated, to make inroads on Christian villages, quarter their horsemen on their inhabitants, until a given sum of money had been extorted, carry off their cattle, their poultry and other provisions, and, in case of remonstrance or resistance, subject them to the most brutal punishments. The Christian women, in many instances, were not free from Druze importunity, though violence was never resorted to.

Among the most wayward, overbearing and

unscrupulous of these feudal marauders, was Said Bey Jumblatt. His grasping and unprincipled covetousness extended even to the direct and open confiscation of landed property, overtaking at times both Druze and Christians alike. His secretary and confidential agent had a bag of forged Christian seals, ready at hand, apparently to facilitate and confer a mock legalisation on the surreptitious transfer of goods or money, or in case of necessity, and for self-defence, to be affixed to testimonials crediting him for general kindness and humanity. His yearly descent into the Bekaa during the harvest was like a razzia. The unfortunate peasants were summoned and forced to deliver up a third of their corn and barley crops at one half of its value, and compelled to carry it, by forced labour, to Muchtara.

On arriving at his granaries, it was measured out in such a manner as to be greatly reduced in bulk, and the price of the deficit was charged to them, at double and compound interest, until the ensuing year. Did any of the unfortunate Christians go down to complain of their hardships to the pasha at Beyrout, their appeals were instantly rendered nugatory, by presents of oil, honey or tobacco, to that authority, on the part of their lawless chiefs. At times the poor wretches would betake themselves to the British consulate, as a tribunal where the right would surely be upheld, oppression struck down, and justice obtained; for Said Bey was under British protection.

But Said Bey was too powerful and important an instrument of political influence, in the eyes of the British government, to be lightly interfered with, and though he might be, and was occasionally remonstrated with, on account of his enormities, yet the one decisive step of breaking with him, and depriving him of the highly privileged connection which he disgraced, was never permitted, if even it was ever entertained. Thus, in this quarter likewise, the Christians became victims to their deluded ideas of obtaining redress. On their return to their homes, they were not unfrequently waylaid by Said Bey's Druzes, and beaten till they fainted, or till the blood poured from their wounds.

Certainly, the perseverance with which the British government continued to countenance and support this Druze chief, notwithstanding his known delinquencies, not only excited the wonder, and most justly, of the Christians, but had a most deteriorating effect on the Druzes themselves. It gave them the most false and erroneous estimate of their own importance in the eyes of that government. It encouraged the whole Druze community in their contempt and disregard for the Christians as a body. It is evident, they argued, that we are preferred to them; the British government, whatever we do, will never discard us or disown us: as for the Christians, they must be of very small importance indeed in its eyes. So strongly did these feelings, and this way of thinking thus apparently sanctioned, exist latterly amongst the Druzes, that during the late massacres many of them absolutely thought they were doing the English a service, by extirpating a sect whose clergy denounced them as heretics, freemasons and infidels.

This general demeanour of the Druzes towards the Christians, so utterly at variance with that displayed by them in the earlier period of their history, can only be accounted for by that exacerbation of feeling, almost inducing a transformation of character, which resulted from the steadily manifested designs and repeated attempts made by the leaders of the Maronites, both lay and clerical, to break up and destroy their confederacy, to weaken their influence, curtail their rights, and finally to get rid of them altogether. The old Emir Beshir Shehab, a Maronite, during his long and ferocious rule over the Lebanon, had almost literally broken them to pieces with a rod of iron. And when at his fall they looked for breathing time and indulged in hopes of better days, again the Maronite clergy presented them with the alternative of submission to their dictates or the sword.

It is not surprising therefore that when the Druze chiefs had once placed their feet firmly on the vantage ground which the new system had given them, with a governor out of their own ranks, themselves in a state of virtual independence, and altogether removed from even the shadow of Christian control, they should have displayed somewhat of that spirit of vindictiveness which is their indelible characteristic, or indulged in those excesses which even amongst more polished natures, are too frequently the consequences of unbridled and irresponsible power.

Notwithstanding, however, the general liberty of action, and almost entire freedom from superior control which the Druzes had acquired, the Christians could still point to and boast of more than one centre of strength and prosperity, which served as rallying points to their hopes, and acted as checks to Druze lawlessness. The towns of Deir-el-Kamar and Zachlé had both been called into existence by the old Emir Beshir Shehab during the latter part of his life, when he was more and more subsiding into the hands of the priesthood, as a counterpoise to the hitherto too exclusive predominance of the Druze commonalty. Deir-el-Kamar is situated in the very heart of the Druze country, about twenty miles from Beyrout and eighteen from Sidon. Its old serail was built by the Emir Fakaradeen Maan, who made it the seat of his government early in the seventeenth century. The Maans had previously occupied Bakleen, on the opposite ridge, a deep valley intervening.

The Shehabs, who succeeded the Maans about the beginning of the eighteenth century, were installed at Deir-el-Kamar, at that time, notwithstanding the importance of its site, a small straggling village inhabited by Druzes. Under the patronage of the Emir Beshir it rose to be an important town with a large Christian population, principally composed of Maronites and Greek Catholics, and amounting latterly to nearly 8000 souls. It became reputed for its silk manufactures. Its merchants built spacious houses, with marble courts and fountains, and furnished in a style of costly luxury. All the Druze landed property in the neighbourhood passed into their hands. Thus they finally attained a position of wealth and affluence which excited the jealousy and cupidity of their feudal superiors, the Druze sheiks of the family of Abou Nakad.

Misled by the ill-judged councils of the Maronite patriarch, they had evinced a disposition to join in the attempts made against Druze supremacy, and thereby entailed upon themselves the rancour and hatred of chiefs who could hardly forgive them a prosperity which, of itself, was galling to their pride. Released from the restraints which had hitherto weighed upon them from that quarter, by being placed under a Turkish governor, the Christians of Deir-el-Kamar enjoyed the full and unimpeded development of commercial activity. Their leading men amassed riches; they kept studs; their wives and daughters were apparelled in silks and satins, and blazed with jewellery, gold, and pearls, and diamonds. The few Druzes who still inhabited the town were reduced to absolute insignificance, were always obliged to be on their good behaviour, and, to use their own expression, often repeated in the bitterness of their hearts, had become to the Christians as "hewers of wood and drawers of water."

In their general intercourse with the Druzes, the Christians of Deir-el-Kamar assumed an air of independence and superiority, commensurate with their privileged emancipation from Druze control. They boasted, with complacency and even with arrogance, of their 2000 warriors, ready on a crisis to compete with three times their number of Druzes, and certainly with justice, if united and properly led. They interfered, and often with effect, in cases of Druze oppression towards Christians throughout the districts around them. The Druzes who repaired to their market place, or to their bazaars, were obliged to wear a demeanour of circumspection and humility. The slightest attempts at wrangling or dispute on their parts were sure to be resented, and promptly put down, sometimes with menaces, sometimes with blows. Even the Druze sheiks, in passing through the town, felt involuntarily crestfallen.

So instinctively did the Christians of Deir-el-Kamar dread any opening which might threaten them with the proximity of their former chiefs, that when Beshir Bey Abou Nakad, only two years ago, wanted to build a house on a piece of ground belonging to him about a mile from the town, they sent to him to desist from his intentions, accompanying their message with the threat, that as fast as he built they would pull down. All negotiations on the subject proved useless; the Christians were inexorable; and the sheik was advised to abandon his design. He did so; but with the savage and, indeed, too prophetic exclamation:— "Those dogs, I will yet lay the foundations of my house with their skulls!"

The town of Zachlé, within the jurisdiction of the kaimmakam of the Christians, and with the exception of a few families of Greek Christians exclusively comprising Greek Catholics, had risen with astonishing rapidity to a state of affluence and consideration. The population amounts to 12,000, of whom the 3000 who bear arms enjoy a considerable reputation, greatly over-rated however, for courage and bravery. Its principal inhabitants carry on a large trade in wool, importing sheep from the north of Syria, which they dispose of in the Lebanon. They farm largely, likewise, in the Bekaa, on the borders of which their town stands, and where they long presented a powerful check to the marauding propensities of the Druzes, too long accustomed to consider that fertile district, with its numerous villages, as a fair field for their robberies and exactions.

They formed a kind of federal alliance with the Christians of Deir-el-Kamar for the general protection of Christian interests, if seriously menaced by the Druzes; who, in their turn, cordially hated them, not indeed without dread, for their lofty pretensions, their invidious prosperity, and the efficient front they presented to their own attempts at tyranny and spoliation.

In the anti-Lebanon the large village of Hasbeya, containing a population of 6000 Greek Christians and scarcely 1500 Druzes, formed another nucleus of Christian strength. The former had never forgiven the conduct of the Druzes towards them when, armed with all the powers of the Turkish government, they had disarmed them, ill-treated them, and subjected them to every species of humiliation. The consequence was a rancorous hostility between the two sects which could never be effaced. The Mohammedan branch of the Shehabs, who were the local governors, were likewise in constant collision with the Druzes, who were ever invading their rights and contesting their authority. It became their policy, therefore, to seek the support of the Christians. The restless encroachments of the Druzes in the surrounding parts, their old resorts in the Wady-el-Tame, their petty intrigues and overt acts of outrage rendered the maintenance of peace and tranquillity utterly impossible, and the Christians were often obliged to stand on the alert like a beleaguered garrison.

When these significant details are borne in mind, the subsequent tragic fate which overtook the Christians in the above-named places, when the Druzes rushed upon them in all the flush and fury of revenge and conquest, will be easily explained.

The Druzes had now obtained a political "status," which left nothing to be desired. All their feudal privileges had been consecrated. Each of their great families reigned supreme in its district. The Christians living amongst them were entirely under their control. Their kaimmakam, with forces at his disposal utterly inadequate to make his authority respected, was content to receive from the sheiks a purely nominal obedience over the latter. The Turkish authorities held no direct jurisdiction whatever. Their orders had to be conveyed through the kaimmakam, and were, consequently, obeyed or not, according to the temper and fancy of those to whom they were transmitted. The Druze confederacy, had, in fact, become like a little independent republic.

It was not long before the effects of such a state of affairs became apparent. As every successive year seemed to assure the Druze sheiks of increased confirmation to their power, and irresponsibility to their actions, they continued to indulge in a freedom and license which set all restraint at defiance. Charged with collecting the imperial revenues, they appropriated them to their own uses. Houses were built, lands purchased, crown property farmed, horses gorgeously caparisoned, all surreptitiously out of the coffers of the state. Though repeatedly called to account, they always contrived to postpone, and then altogether to evade, the day of reckoning. If their kaimmakam, in despair at these long arrears of taxes, for which he alone was answerable to the government, ventured to send horsemen amongst them intreating even an instalment, be it ever so small, of their dues, they were either allowed free quarters until, tired with bootless expectation, they took their departure; or, in case of disagreeable pertinacity, unceremoniously ejected.

At the commencement of the Russian war, the Druze sheiks volunteered their services to raise a force, and go to the Crimea or to Asia Minor. They were loud in their protestations of loyalty to the Sultan and of hatred to the infidel. The Turkish authorities determined to try them, and devoted 150,000*l.* for their especial use. The sheiks came down from their mountain abodes with great pomp and parade, followed by hundreds of Druzes, floating their banners and singing their war-songs, each to receive the portion allotted to him for pay and equipment. But here their patriotism ended. Having pocketed the money, they loitered about the country under various pretences for several months, and ended by never leaving it all. The government made repeated demands for an account of the large sums thus fraudulently obtained from them, but without the slightest avail.

Throughout the Druze districts life and property became, by degrees, equally insecure. The Druzes robbed and murdered whom they pleased with perfect impunity. Within a term of ten years upwards of seven hundred murders were committed within their jurisdiction, without causing even an attempt at investigation or inquiry. In one atrocious case of a whole Christian family having been slaughtered in cold blood by the Druzes, representations were made to Constantinople, and three successive vizierial letters formally ordered Kurchid Pasha to take immediate measures for discovering and punishing the perpetrators of the crime. No notice whatever was taken of them. The Druzes gloried openly in their deed; and the unhappy Christians felt that they were bound over hand and foot to the knives of their assassins, whenever it might please the latter to draw them.

Let it not be supposed that there existed not the power to check these savage and lawless depredations. It required no great display of military force to reduce the Druzes to absolute subjection, or to enable the government to recover from them all their claims of whatever kind or nature. The slightest moral support given by the Turks to the Druze kaimmakam, in the execution of his duties, but given in such a manner as to have let the Druzes feel that it emanated from an earnest and determined will, and might be followed up, if necessary, by a correspondent vigour of action, would have amply sufficed to chastise their insolent defiance of all the laws of right and justice, and to rescue the Christians from their intolerable tyranny and oppression.

But such was neither the object nor the policy of the Turks in the Lebanon. Not being allowed to rule it in their own manner, they took a spiteful satisfaction in seeing it laid waste by anarchy and disorder. They hoped, indeed they felt assured, that the inevitable crisis must come, when the two sects would again stand opposed to each other in hostile array, when they might once more play their own desperate game; and thus they granted an unlimited indulgence to the Druzes, in all their wilful acts and wayward caprices, even to the extent of demeaning themselves before them, in order that, when the hour arrived, they might find in them willing and cheerful instruments for the accomplishment of their own nefarious designs.

The triumphant issue of the Russian war was peculiarly trying to the egotism and self-sufficiency of the Turks. They felt that they had just owed their salvation, and their national existence, to the generous intervention of powers whose religion they despised and whose liberalism they detested. The very fact that they required such assistance was revolting to their pride. How to maintain their own importance in the eyes of their Mohammedan subjects, under such extraordinary ties of obligation and gratitude, became in their eyes a consideration of paramount importance: the more so, as there was one of these powers at least, which had determined that such a costly expenditure of blood and treasure on its part, should not have been laid out without obtaining something in return, bordering on a commensurate advantage to the rayahs scattered throughout, more especially, the eastern provinces of their empire.

And it must be confessed that the attitude assumed by France, at this epoch, towards them, must have largely tried their patience, as it undoubtedly increased and embittered all their feelings of sectarian hatred. Throughout Syria, in particular, the French consular authorities suddenly assumed an air of supervision over

Christian interests, as pre-eminently theirs by prescriptive right, which had for years lain apparently dormant. The French consul-general at Beyrout became distinguished more than any of his colleagues, for his lofty assumptions, his dictatorial bearing, and his patriotic desire to extend French influence. Of his sincere and well-intentioned hopes of bettering and elevating the prospects of the Christians by such fearless conduct, and of his actually succeeding, more or less, in vindicating to them, for the moment, an eligible position, there cannot be a doubt. But his zeal was without knowledge. He loved the Christian cause, " not wisely but too well."

The sense of self-complacent security, and even of superiority, which the Christians under his ostentatious protection entertained, and their haughty and arrogant defiance of all authority but his, would have been vastly pleasant and desirable for them, if it could have lasted ; and the idea of its not lasting, of course never once entered their protector's mind. " He that of old would rend the oak," " dreamt not of the rebound." And he whose whole course of proceeding seemed like a deliberate crusade against Mohammedan antipathies and Mohammedan susceptibilities, never appeared to reflect for one moment that he was thereby supplying the springs to an under-current of fierce and deadly fanaticism, which, however overborne and kept out of sight for the time, would be ready on the slightest occasion or opportunity to rise to the surface with an impetus almost resistless and overwhelming.

Not a thing was left undone by the French consul-general which could excite the jealousy and malignity of the Turkish authorities, and of their co-religionists, though certainly not with that intent. The former quailed submissively before his presumed influence at Constantinople, and trembled for their places. They yielded at once to all his dictates. The prison doors were closed or opened at his will. Agas and mutsellims were appointed or displaced at his sovereign pleasure. Mohammedans in the public wayfares were compelled to stand still, or to rise up, at the approach of the august presence.

French protégés, or the sons, or the cousins of protégés were amenable to him alone, sat down on the pasha's divan as with an equal, and treated his officers with utter disdain. Arab emirs from the most distant tribes, Druze, Anserian and Christian sheiks alike, were politely invited to attend the French durbar, there to receive the great man's behests, revel in his sunshine, and drink of the fountain of rewards and emoluments. At times, he would make a tour through the mountain, where his reception was a perfect ovation, with ringing of church and convent bells, processions of priests, and blazing of musketry.

No wonder if the Turks gazed on this fleshly apparition with fear, wonder and amazement. Or, that viewing his constant and intimate relations with the Christians of the Lebanon, his lordly missions to their kaimmakam, his secret conferences with the Maronite patriarch, they thought the time had come at last when the Lebanon was to be made an outpost for the introduction of a foreign power into their land.

On the Mussulman masses the sensation created by the aspiring and even domineering aspect which the Christians were thus assuming was immense. Every post that went out from Beyrout carried letters to the most distant parts of Syria, depicting in fervent terms the degraded and fallen condition of the faithful, and the insults to which they were daily exposed by the meanest giaour who could glory in the immunity of Frank protection. Jerusalem, Aleppo, Damascus, all likewise had their responsive tales of humiliation and wrong. In the latter city, — the holy and almost divine, from whence Mohammed turned aside as too transcendent for his presence, where Jesus is to descend in person to judge the world, where the standards of the Infidel had never yet been planted, and where Christianity itself ever bowed down in meekness and humility before the unsullied sceptre of Islam, — native Christians had become merchant princes, lived in palaces resplendent with gilt and marble, flaunted their wealth, sported their gorgeous finery, and indulged in every species of expense and luxury. And while thus exciting the deep felt jealousy and craving cupidity of their less fortunate Mohammedan neighbours, the latter had recently been compelled to behold some of them elevated to the rank of representatives of European powers; and men, whom but a few years before, on meeting, they would have unceremoniously elbowed into the kennel, now strutted before them through the bazaars, preceded by all the paraphernalia of consular dignity, and with more than consular pretension.

In this state of things Mohammedanism, in all parts of Syria, began to stand, as it were, on the defensive. Secret societies were everywhere formed. By every means, and by any means, the progress of the general degradation was to be stopped. If the seat of the evil was at Constantinople, where a weak, wavering, and too complacent Sultan was criminally yielding up, one by one, the brightest prerogatives of the apostolic mission, and languidly consenting, at Frank dictation, to the surrender of those distinctive and dearly cherished rights, glorious guerdons of that true faith which the sword had achieved and time had consecrated, let his life be taken, and a worthier scion of the Prophet invested with the sacred mantle. Or, that failing, let all true believers henceforward look to their own right arms, await the hour, and stand ready for the sign,—

"Awake, arise, or be for ever fallen!"

Such was undoubtedly the universally pervading Mohammedan spirit throughout the Ottoman empire in 1857, as it is to this hour, and by none more deeply entertained or more warmly fomented, than by the Turks themselves.

About this time, and consequent on the death of his predecessor, they got into the post of kaimmakam of the Christians of the Lebanon, the well tried and approved agent of their corruption and intrigues, the Emir Beshir Abou Lamá. The ball was now at their feet, and nothing was wanting but patience and dexterity to bring about the accomplishment of their views. Whatever might have been the obligation of the new kaimmakam to his patrons, or his compact with the pasha at Beyrout, he was soon made to feel that there was another functionary who claimed his allegiance and demanded his submission. The ever active, zealous, and indefatigable French consul-general, also aspired, as well as the Turk, to the direct and undivided control of the Lebanon; and the kaimmakam found himself apparently in a dilemma. He soon discovered, however, that his difficulty was not insurmountable. Of him it could not have been said, "Ye cannot serve two masters," for he served both the one and the other with perfect consistency —the action of both leading to turbulence and anarchy.

The effects of French consular pressure on the kaimmakam were not long in making themselves felt. The latter, a Druze by birth, as were originally the whole of his family, held a profession almost nominal, of the Christian faith; and certainly, by sentiment and inclination, sympathised but little with the bigoted idiosyncracies of the Maronite priesthood. The Maronite patriarch was not his idol. Yet was he made to fall down and worship. He bound himself by oath, in the presence of the French consul-general, to obey its slightest nod. A triumvirate was thus established, animated by two principles,—submission of the civil to the ecclesiastical power, and exclusive devotion of both to France. Whoever contravened or thwarted the carrying out of this programme was to be ruthlessly crushed.

The Maronite patriarch, at this epoch, who had likewise been recently installed into his office, was remarkable for two things;— hatred to the feudal aristocracy, and a fanatic devotion to the religious tenets of his own sect. For centuries back, the Maronite patriarchs had, almost without exception, been selected from one or other of the leading noble families in the Lebanon. He was a peasant, a feudal dependent of the ancient family of Haazin, to whom he was wholly indebted for his education, his subsequent gradations in the priestly office, and even for his accession to the patriarchate itself. All the feelings of obligation, however, which such benefits might otherwise have produced, were merged in the promptings of innate intolerance, and of that inherent aversion to superior rank and station, which, more particularly in the feudal system, is apt to be engendered in the breast of a man of the people.

Ere long the Maronite aristocracy found the kaimmakam invading their rights, assailing their privileges, and assuming the exercise of his own direct functions in matters which had for ages been referred to them alone. The Greek Christians again became the objects of an invidious proselytism. On one occasion a Greek Christian in a large and populous village of that sect, having become a Maronite, the church was claimed for the Maronite ritual; its officiating priest was brutally assaulted at the altar; the kaimmakam quartered horseman on the recusants to compel a surrender, and finally it was converted into a stable. In cases of legal procedure at the civil tribunal, the claims of Greek Christians were uniformly neglected, and their rights in cases of litigation with Maronites unscrupulously ignored. If they remonstrated they were rudely ejected; if they complained, they were assaulted and beaten.

The natural consequence of such proceedings was a general feeling of excitement and discontent throughout the Maronite districts of the Lebanon. The aggrieved parties came down in bodies to Beyrout to complain to Kurchid Pasha. Sometimes they were waylaid and attacked by the creatures of the kaimmakam, and if any were seized, they were taken up to his residence in the mountain and thrown into chains. The pasha received them with coldness, and even with derision. Their petitions were declared to be factious. Such an expression of public dislike to a constituted authority was denounced as rebellious, and the petitioners soon discovered the futility of their hopes of redress. They made representations to Constantinople with greater effect, and Lord Stratford de Redcliffe, with that sterling energy which ever distinguished all his relations with the Porte, compelled it to send down an express commission to Syria for the purposes of investigation.

Like all Turkish special commissions, especially those extorted by European remonstrance, the mission proved a wilful failure. The commissioner played into the hands of the local authorities, was himself largely bribed, signed a report drawn up by those very authorities, that the kaimmakam was perfectly blameless, and the complainants insolent rebels; and after a few months' absence returned to Constantinople. Never was a more notorious case of intrigue, corruption and injustice than this affair presented. But the Turks would not hear of removing their tool. An honest kaimmakam would have been an obstacle in their path. Their object was to show that no government but their own could possibly succeed in the Lebanon, and the more the Lebanon plunged into disorder and confusion, the nearer they hoped they were to its attainment. The European powers, they reasoned, would get wearied with these perpetual scenes of agitation, civil strife and bloodshed, and at last yield the point.

In the mean time, the triumvirate had issued its mandates. The Haazin sheiks, rulers of the populous district of the Kesrouan, had committed the unpardonable offence of seeking the support of the British government to the representation of their grievances at the Porte. This glaring departure on their parts, from the principle of Maronite allegiance to France, could not only be not overlooked, but to prevent the bad example spreading, must be signally chastised. All of a sudden their peasants rose against them in armed insurrection. The kaimmakam had distinctly told them to murder their sheiks and seize their property; and the hint was promptly taken.

Armed bodies moved about in every direction, menacing the sheiks with instant death. The latter had to fly for their lives, and escaped with the greatest difficulty, though not without wounds. A few took refuge in the patriarch's palace. The mob pursued them, surrounded the building, and loudly called for them to be delivered up. The patriarch pretended his utter inability to stem the torrent, affected to parley with the insurgents, and finally gave the unfortunate sheiks an escort to Beyrout.

The movement ended in the establishment of a regularly organised jacquerie, who proceeded to every species of agrarian outrage. The houses of the ejected sheiks were burnt to the ground. One of them was found in concealment. He was instantly seized, a rope was put about his neck, he was dragged about in wanton sport, and then trampled to death. His wife and daughter were at the same time massacred. The whole of their property was confiscated, their woods cut down and distributed for common usage.

During the whole of 1858 and 1859 the process of robbery and plunder went fearlessly on. The peasants elected a dictator, to whom they pledged a blind obedience; and he in his turn appointed leaders to do his bidding, and an executive committee to regulate judicial proceedings, and take cognisance of acts of disobedience. Emboldened by impunity, they declared their emancipation from all superior power, turned against the kaimmakam himself, and told him they cared neither for him nor his Turkish master. And, in effect, on the Pasha once sending an officer accompanied by some troops to remonstrate with them, they defied him to advance one step into their mountains on pain of being driven back, and scornfully scouted all his propositions.

The Haazins in their despair scarcely knew from what quarter to expect relief. The Turkish authorities remained callously indifferent to their wrongs. The French consul-general and the patriarch were their avowed enemies. All their hope rested on the generous sympathy and powerful support of the British government, to whom they pleaded their former services in 1840, when the British fleet had appeared off the coast, and summoned them to a co-operation against the

Egyptian forces. They adduced the solemn guarantees it had given them that their privileges should be preserved, their prescriptive rights confirmed, and their ancient usages respected. The British government, they rightly argued, was bound by every sentiment of justice and honour to insist with the Porte that measures should be taken for the signal punishment of their spoliators and assassins, and for their own restoration to their properties and homes. These urgent appeals were conveyed in sundry petitions to the British embassy at Constantinople. But all in vain. There the master mind that could, and would, have rectified and controlled, was gone. England's new ambassador " cared little for these things," or, if he did, his will was weak and his voice inefficient. A zealous supporter of the doctrine of " non-intervention," so suicidal to the maintenance of British influence and the vindication of British interests throughout the Ottoman empire, and so fatal even to the welfare of that empire itself, the Turkish ministers were left to follow their own dark devices, and to pursue without a guide their blind and infatuated career.

The Turks, in their selfish fanaticism, beheld with secret satisfaction an accumulation of circumstances which promised at no distant period to throw the Lebanon into their hands. The Christians had assumed an attitude which they felt, and hoped, would outleap all bounds of moderation and discretion. They knew that as their turbulence augmented their aspirations would increase. They had expressly countenanced a turbulence with that view, hoping to lead them on to their ruin. They might at any time have restored order. But such was not their object. To have reduced the Christians to obedience, while the Druzes were in a state of virtual independence, would have been no gain to them. It is questionable which of the two sects they most cordially detested, the one for their feudal arrogance, or the other for their hated creed. But by embroiling them both, and making the one their instrument for utterly crushing the other, even at the risk of outraging all the best feelings of humanity, both might eventually become their victims. Then, indeed, they would be masters of the situation. The time had now arrived which seemed eminently propitious to the consummation of their views.

The Druze sheiks were consequently taken into especial favour. Whenever they came down from their mountain abodes, they were received in the most flattering manner. Some were made confidential agents, others obtained lucrative commands. Said Bey Jumblatt, their most influential chief, received a firman from Constantinople appointing him an Imperial equerry, with a decoration. A few of them, who used to frequent certain consulates, were taunted with their disloyal leanings to foreign powers. Where could they find a more generous and beneficial protection than in their own Sultan, who was now the uncontrolled master of his own policy, totally exempt from all foreign dictation or interference, and accountable to no one for his actions? Finding themselves thus courted, with their barefaced appropriation of the public revenues overlooked, their various malversations to escape responsibility successful, and their constant outrages upon life and property condoned, the Druzes naturally entertained most exaggerated ideas of their own importance, and at the same time slavishly propitiated the patronage of their too indulgent masters. The Turks having thus laid their plans had only to wait patiently the course of events.

CHAP. V.

Affray, August 1859.—Kurchid Pasha.—War Preparations.—Druze Aggression, May 1860.—Defeat of the Christians at Aindara.—Druze military Superiority.—Onslaught of the Druzes, May 30, 1860.—Villages plundered.—Deir-el-Kamar invested and taken.—Massacre of 1200 Maronites in Jezeen.—Plunder of Convents.—Druze Resolve to slaughter every male adult Christian.—June 1860, Hasbeya.—The Turkish Garrison.—The Christians located in the Grand Quadrangle.—June 3, the Druze female Demon, Sitt Naaify, takes Hasbeya.—June 4, Rascheya taken.—The Christians of Karaoon.—The Massacre at Hasbeya.—Sitt Naaify feasts on the mangled Corpses of the butchered Christians.

On the 30th of August, 1859, a serious affray took place between the Druzes and Maronites in the village of Bate-mirri, three hours distant, in the mountain, from Beyrout. The original cause was a quarrel between a Druze and Christian boy. The father of the latter, afterwards with three other Maronites, reproached the father of the Druze boy, and insisted that he should chastise his son. The Druze informed his relations, who, greatly excited, sent for reinforcements of Druzes from neighbouring villages, and the following morning assembled together and demanded an apology for the insult. The Maronites were about to accede to the request, when some Druzes fired off their muskets as a bravado. The former, mistaking this for a challenge, rushed to arms, and fired a general volley on the Druzes, following it up by a vigorous attack. The Druzes were driven out of the village with great loss. The next day, a Sunday, the Druzes rallied; a desperate encounter, which lasted all the day, ensued between the two sects, and the Christians were in their turn defeated. On the whole, however, the Druzes had lost in killed twenty-eight more than the Christians, who on this occasion had displayed unusual bravery.

The Turkish authorities were evidently taken by surprise. An officer was immediately sent to the village, who secured the principal offenders on both sides, and effected an apparent reconciliation. The Druzes, nevertheless, in other parts of the mountain, had taken the affray as a signal for civil war. Writhing under their unexpected defeat and heavy loss, they had already, under the guidance of one of their sheiks, commenced burning some Christian villages, when Kurchid Pasha, informed of the serious aspect which matters had assumed, rode up to a central position on the Damascus road, accompanied by a few soldiers, to stop the further progress of the evil. He there summoned the chiefs of both parties to his presence, and peremptorily enjoined them to keep the peace. Order was at once re-established. But the Druzes who had committed the outrages above mentioned were neither punished nor arrested. The power of the Turks over the mountaineers to enforce obedience to their commands, was thus clearly demonstrated. Here had been no necessity for artillery, or cavalry, or thousands of troops to separate the combatants. Civil war, at that moment, did not suit their purpose. They willed that hostilities should cease — and they ceased.

All who knew the temper of the rival sects, and the passions by which they were animated, saw that civil war between them, notwithstanding its temporary suspension, was from henceforward merely a question of time. The Maronites had been animated and encouraged by their first victory. If those of Bate-mirri, never famous for their courage, had inflicted such a loss upon the Druzes, what might not be expected from the Christians of Deir-el-Kamar, of Zachlé, of Gezeen, if they drew their swords? That the Druzes, on their part, could ever sincerely forgive, and forget their sanguinary defeat, or abandon all thoughts of retaliation, was impossible. And, in fact, from this date, both sides began to look upon a deadly contest as inevitable, and to prepare themselves accordingly.

The sudden appeal to arms thus made by the Druzes, for a very slight provocation, and the rapidity with which they had united from various distant parts, clearly evincing preconcerted designs, threw the Christian population into general alarm. For the last fifteen years the Druzes had been oppressing the Christians living amongst them in every possible manner. A Christian could hardly call his life his own. A widely spread feeling of commiseration for their degraded and unhappy lot had become general throughout the Lebanon. The Jumblatts, the Amads and the Abou Nakads were pre-eminent for their barbarous and unfeeling despotism. A considerable check on their lawless proceedings, however, was to be found in the Christian strongholds, to which allusion has already been made; and for this reason, they longed for an occasion to attack, spoliate, and destroy them. The better to cover their insidious and unprincipled designs, they always talked loudly of their desire to keep the peace, constantly denounced the Maronites as reckless agitators, and adroitly repeated, and put prominently forward, the violent expressions they had used against themselves at a former period.

As the Mohammedans in the towns invariably prefaced and excused their attacks upon the Christians by raising reports that they were about to be attacked by them; so the Druzes became more and more vehement in their denunciations of Christian aggression, in proportion as the time approached for crushing and utterly eradicating the few vestiges of Christian strength which still offered them an imposing front, in what they haughtily and superbly designated, the "mountains of the Druzes."

The Christians seeing clearly through all these hypocritical manifestations, and marking with secret dread the intimacy and close alliance which existed between the Druzes and the Turkish authorities, naturally began to take measures for self-defence. Maronites of wealth and means raised subscriptions for the purpose of purchasing arms and ammunition, which they distributed to their co-religionists in the mountains. A general desire was evinced to merge all sectarian differences between them and the Greek Christians, in order to effect a thorough union and co-operation throughout the Christian body. The Maronite clergy lent the whole weight of their influence to achieve so desirable a consummation. The Christians had hitherto been feeble through their mutual jealousies. At such a period as the present, when there was evidently a conspiracy organising against their common faith;— a dark design, premeditated and even ill-disguised, to throw their whole race into a state of abject servitude, by letting loose upon them the ferocious passions of the Druzes, the necessity for combined action was indispensable, and each should be ready at his post when the hour of trial came. Such was the language of the Maronites.

The Turks, on their parts, who perfectly well knew the prevalence of such sentiments, and saw the extensive preparations which accompanied them, proceeded to draw closer the relations which already existed between them and the Druzes. Several Druze sheiks took the unusual step of spending the winter of 1859—60 at Beyrout. Here, their conferences with the Turkish authorities were long and frequent, and almost of daily occurrence. Of the object of those meetings there could be no possible doubt; and though all the minuter details discussed, remained of course unknown, the great fact transpired, that the Druzes had been called upon to prepare themselves for a most responsible and important service, that they had responded to the call in terms of absolute devotion to the Sultan, but had taken the liberty to observe that such responsibilities could not be undertaken, or such services entered upon, without explicit sanction, and clear and definite instructions from Constantinople. Early in the spring of 1860 they returned to their homes.

In the month of April, Kurchid Pasha received despatches from Constantinople which seemed suddenly to relieve him from a disagreeable suspense. His language displayed a tone of buoyancy and assurance. It was even rumoured about the serail, that a firman had arrived which would soon bring the giaours to their senses. Shortly afterwards, Said Bey Jumblatt assembled a Druze divan at Much̄tara. His correspondence became unintermitting. His chief adherents came pouring in from all quarters. A fortnight later, a general agitation prevailed throughout the Druze districts of the Lebanon. Isolated Christians, sometimes even parties of Christians, were attacked and assassinated by the Druzes, on the high roads, which were more or less intercepted in every direction. Seized with consternation and alarm, whole families of Christians now abandoned their villages and sought refuge in such central places of resort as Zach̄lé and Deir-el-Kamar. The houses of the fugitives were in many instances burnt to the ground. They were not unfrequently, however, overtaken by the Druzes, who, at the very least, robbed, wounded and disarmed them. By way of a deeper insult, and more surely calculated to create excitement and provoke retaliation, as touching the religious susceptibilities of the Christians, some Druzes, on the 4th of May, broke into the Maronite convent of Ameek, near Deir-el-Kamar, and murdered the superior in his bed.

In the village of Hasbeya, the Druzes, under the direction of Sitt Naaify, sister of Said Bey Jumblatt, from whom she received her orders, began to clear out their houses, removing all their furniture to other places; and this three weeks before an actual collision had anywhere occurred between the Druzes and the Christians. In vain the Christians asked the meaning of all these movements, earnestly expressing their wishes to remain at peace, and even sending their leaders to the Druze ockals, imploring them to use their good offices to arrest the impending rupture; they were met with subtle excuses, assurances of the needlessness of their alarms, and other reasons equally specious. They went so far, at last, as to propitiate the ockals with costly presents in linen and cloth, besides the ordinary offerings of rice, coffee, sugar, &c., ready, in fact, to sacrifice anything, in order, if possible, to avoid a civil war. An apparent reconciliation was momentarily effected, but the Druze preparations went on with unabated vigour.

The Christians in the mixed districts, seeing themselves thus menaced on all sides, felt that the hour of trial had arrived. A few reprisals were made on their parts, but nothing to be compared with the ferocity of the attacks which had been made upon them. Some Druzes descending into the plains of Beyrout were stopped and disarmed. The Christians in the highlands, under the Druze sheik Amad, alarmed at the increasing forces assembled at Mu*c*htara, in their immediate vicinity, left their villages in a body, about the 21st of May, and fled towards the Bekaa, intending to make for Za*c*hlé. They were vigorously pursued and fired upon.

There could now be no farther doubt as to the nature of the Druze aggression, and the Christians of the Lebanon, in self-defence, took up the gauntlet of defiance. On the 27th of May, the men of Za*c*hlé advanced, 3000 strong, to attack the Druze village of Aindara. They were encountered by 600 Druzes led on by their sheiks, on the Damascus road, when the first regular conflict between the two sects took place. The battle raged all day, and ended in the complete discomfiture of the Christians, who retreated in the utmost confusion. The Druzes rapidly followed up their success, and spread into the neighbouring district of the Metten, where they were equally successful, and burnt down some Christian villages. Throughout the remainder of the civil war, which lasted altogether about a month, this district was the scene of constant encounter between the hostile parties, with alternate success, until all its villages, amounting to more than sixty, had been entirely destroyed.

The inferiority of the Christians in military organisation to that of the Druzes, became apparent, as usual, from the first collision. The former advanced without the slightest order, dispersed themselves right and left, and seemed each to follow his own inspirations. In the battle near Aindara, they actually fired upon each other, and while thus engaged, found themselves outflanked, and nearly surrounded by the enemy. The Druzes, on the contrary, moved steadily on given points, under the direction of their chiefs, to whom they yielded the most implicit obedience. Quarters menaced were carefully watched, and if attacked, reinforced with extraordinary celerity.

And herein consists the whole of the superiority of the Druzes over the Christians in the field. Their arrangements and their discipline are better. The Druze chiefs are personally more daring than those of the Christians, but the commonalty of both sects in this respect are much on a par. If the Christians had good leaders, and could be imbued with the spirit of discipline, the Druzes would have nothing to boast of. The latter have acquired a fictitious reputation for extraordinary courage and bravery, immensely exaggerated, purely from the tactical deficiencies of their rivals.

Long before the general outbreak, Kurchid Pasha had fixed a camp of Turkish troops, in person, just beyond the pine wood immediately contiguous to Beyrout, and commanding the adjoining plains. There he remained, like a general coolly awaiting his daily reports. No attempt was made now, as on a former occasion, to separate the combatants. On the 28th of May, the insurgent Maronites of the Kesrouan, fearing for the fate of their co-religionists in the village of Baabda and Hadet, the residence of the Shehab emirs, an hour's distance from Beyrout, sent a body of three hundred men to protect them. These passed within gunshot of the camp, without the slightest molestation. On the 29th, however, the pasha sent emissaries to the emirs, calling upon them to send back the reinforcements they had received, and assuring them solemnly of his protection from any attack on the part of the Druzes: a protection which from his vicinity to them he could the more readily afford. His orders were immediately obeyed. The reinforcements withdrew; but most of the male inhabitants having little confidence in such assurances withdrew also. Their presentiments were too fully verified.

On the morning of the 30th of May, the Druzes, by a preconcerted understanding with the

Turks, and even acting by signal, descended from the heights immediately over the above mentioned, and now abandoned villages, and commenced a furious onslaught. Meeting of course with little or no resistance, their raid was quickly accomplished. In less than three hours, the villages were in flames. The Christians, men, women, and children, fled in the utmost consternation. One hundred Turkish soldiers had been previously placed in such a position as to support the Druzes, in case, by any chance, of a reverse, and these now joined the latter in following up the fugitives.

The Turkish irregular cavalry also joined vigorously in the pursuit, cutting down every Christian they overtook, and robbing and plundering the women whom the Druzes had left unmolested. The Turks began the work of incendiarism long before the Druzes arrived. The latter were pushing their way on to Beyrout itself, but three discharges of cannon from the pasha's camp intimated to them that the work expected of them was done. The Druze chiefs dismounted at the pasha's tent, and were received with hearty congratulations.

The loss of the Christians, in life, had not been considerable; but the amount of property destroyed was immense. The silk crops, comprising thousands of okes of cocoons had been either carried off or burnt. The following days were spent by the Druzes in removing their plunder. Mules, donkeys, and even oxen, were put into requisition for this purpose, with all the coolness of a legal proceeding. On the same night, hundreds of Maronites, with their families, flying from the Druze mountains and coming towards Beyrout by the sea shore, for greater safety, were suddenly intercepted by the Druzes and Turks, and cut to pieces; the latter sparing neither woman nor child. The gardens around Beyrout now became hourly thronged with masses of unhappy fugitives, lying about under the trees in all directions, some bleeding, some naked, all in the last stage of destitution. The charitable zeal of the European residents was now actively displayed, and even some respectable Mohammedans administered to the necessities of the unfortunate wretches.

The European consuls-general seeing the Lebanon thus plunged into all the horrors of a civil war, and justly alarmed by the strange conduct of Kurchid Pasha, proceeded in a body to his camp on the 1st of June, and made such representations as they thought most likely to awake him to a sense of his duty. He expressed his anxious desire to suppress the hostilities, vehemently denounced what he called the committee, established at Beyrout, for buying and distributing arms to the Christians, as the cause of the war; threatened even to arrest its members, and concluded by requesting the consuls to do all in their power to restrain the Maronites from sending assistance to their countrymen, declaring that he on his part would give orders to the Druzes to cease from their warfare.*

The consuls were only too ready to give their adhesion to a mutual action which, if faithfully performed by both parties, would at once have

* Papers relating to disturbances in Syria, 1860.

secured the establishment of peace; and they promised to use their utmost influence in the manner the pasha required. The latter had adroitly and wickedly gained a vital point. Making use of the representatives of the European powers as his tools, he had neutralised the general combination and onward movement of the Christian body, which might even yet have rallied and made a good resistance. He took good care, however, to send no such orders as he had promised, to the Druzes, who pursued uninterruptedly their blood-thirsty career.

Said Bey Jumblatt had by this time assumed the command of the Druze forces throughout all the mountain ranges over which he directly or indirectly ruled. The Druzes, in general, had formed a very erroneous and exaggerated idea of the power which the Christians might bring to bear upon them in the present crisis, and were greatly alarmed at their own position. They knew the Christians residing amongst them to be every whit as brave as themselves. They saw the resources which had been for months past lavishly expended in supplying them with arms and ammunition. They knew the unceasing efforts which the Maronite clergy and Maronite leaders had long been making to bring about a cordial agreement and brotherly love between the Christians of all sects, efforts which they believed had been more or less successful; and they thus thought it not improbable that they, scarcely 12,000 in number, might have to contend with 50,000 Christian warriors, rushing on them from all parts, and animated by a spirit of energy and union wholly foreign to them in previous conflicts.

The Druzes felt, however, that there was one potent engine which, if skilfully used in their hands, would amply compensate for their disparity in numbers, — treachery. And they used it perseveringly and triumphantly to the end. Besides, they knew the Turks were at their backs, and would always stand them good in case of need. In order to strengthen his hands, Said Bey called in the Druzes of the Houran, about four days' journey from the Lebanon. Writing to Ismail-il-Uttrush, their great chief, he depicted in the most heartrending terms the awful calamities which had overtaken his faithful and devoted Druzes. Their habitations had been laid waste with fire and sword, their women had been violated, their children had been torn asunder by the ferocious Christians. In the name of God, for the sake of their common religion, let him advance at once to the rescue, or the Druzes as a people would be exterminated. This notable letter, after it was written, was burnt at the four corners, to show the imminence of the danger,—the sign of unutterable despair.

Ismail-il-Uttrush and his Druzes, on the receipt of this terrible appeal, sprung like tigers from their lairs, and, girding on their swords, swore to whet their fangs in the blood of their merciless and unsparing foes.

The chief attention of the Druzes had been for some time directed towards Deir-el-Kamar, whither large numbers of Christians from neighbouring villages had already fled for refuge. The people of that town, believing themselves to be under the especial supervision of their Turkish governor and of the Turkish garrison at his disposal, had vainly imagined that the tide of war would pass them harmless by. Their men had been attacked; one of them had been assassinated; but they generously wrote to the Druzes that so anxious were they to remain on good terms with them, that they would overlook these aggressions. The latter, while expressing an equal desire on their parts to preserve the peace, kept hovering around the place like birds of prey.

Towards the end of May the Christians of Deir-el-Kamar were surprised, on essaying to go out into the country, to find that their town was in a state of blockade. Druze outposts met them at every turn. The roads were intercepted, and their supplies were cut off. The corn in the surrounding fields had been reaped and carried away. Credulously relying on Druze professions of friendship, and on the protection of the Turks, they had made not the slightest preparations for war. They had even refused to listen to appeals sent to them from different quarters, and especially from the Maronite bishop, Toubyah, to join the common cause, to rise in the general defence. "The brave men of Deir-el-Kamar were the right arm of the Christians; would they consent to stand passive spectators of the slaughter of their co-religionists?" To all these remonstrances they invariably replied that they meant to stand perfectly neutral; that they were in an exceptional position; and that, being under the very eyes, as it were, of the Turkish government, it would be useless, as well as unbecoming in them to draw the sword. When, therefore, the storm suddenly gathered round them, they found themselves perplexed, and utterly at variance with each other how to act. They had not even three days' provisions. Famine stared them in the face.

At last the tempest burst. Early on the morning of the 1st of June the forces of the Jumblatts, the Abou Nakads, the Amads, and the Hamadis, amounting to 4000 men, poured down upon the town in furious onset. The inhabitants had barely time to barricade the principal avenues. Behind the works thus hastily thrown up they made a desperate defence. The battle raged till sunset, the Christians gallantly keeping their enemies at bay, and inflicting on them a considerable loss: upwards of one hundred were killed besides large numbers wounded. They themselves only lost twelve. Several Turkish soldiers belonging to the garrison fought in the Druze ranks. The Turkish governor refused to interfere. His men crowded to the serail, and from its ramparts enjoyed the scene. Even of the Christians only one half were engaged, — those in the immediate vicinity of the point of attack. The other half refused to join, and even withheld the necessary supplies of ammunition from their comrades. Treason had done its work. Some had already held secret communication with the Abou Nakads, their ancient lords. Many thought, by maintaining a passive attitude, to secure the peculiar favour of the Turks. Thus, even in the extremity of their distress, the Christians were wavering and divided.

The next day Deir-el-Kamar surrendered to the Druzes. The elders of the Christians made their submission in person to the Druze sheiks. On the 3rd of June Tahir Pasha arrived from Beyrout with 400 soldiers. The Druze sheiks met him at the outskirts of the town, and there held a conference. After the surrender the Druzes burned down 130 houses, and then withdrew.

The pasha then proceeded to the serail, and assembled the leading Christians. Vehemently upbraiding them, he called them rebels, intriguers, and disturbers of the public peace; he knew, he said, that their object was to bring in the French; told them that what was happening to them was a just chastisement for their insubordination, and he hoped they would stand corrected by the wholesome lesson. In answer to their protestations of innocence he replied: "The past is forgiven: henceforward you are under the safe protection of my government. Resume your ordinary occupations. Fear nothing. Deir-el-Kamar is as safe as Constantinople."

The Christians were allowed to keep their arms, but not to stir out of the town. Convoys of mules carrying flour were sent up to them from Beyrout. They were frequently, however, intercepted by the Druzes. Sufficient only reached its destination to enable the Christians to keep body and soul together. What little corn they had was useless. The Druzes had cut off the supplies of water. The mills in the town could not work. The pasha remained at his post nearly a fortnight, and then, notwithstanding the earnest entreaties of the Christians, returned to Beyrout. But, during the whole of his stay, daily assassinations took place ; for whenever a Christian showed his face beyond the town, he was instantly cut down. Many asked permission to leave, but were sternly refused.

Simultaneously with the attack on Deir-el-Kamar, Said Bey Jumblatt had commenced a more extended scale of operations. On the morning of that day a messenger, bearing a letter from him, entered the populous Maronite district of Jezeen. The Maronites were immediately convoked to hear it read. It solemnly assured them of his good will and friendship. They were his children. He pledged himself that no harm should overtake them. Let them attend to their silk crops, nothing dreading. If anything happened to them, he was the responsible person ; he was the Druze power. The Druzes, without his orders, dared not move. And the messenger left the place, carrying a letter of acknowledgment and thanks from the inhabitants for such disinterested generosity.

He had barely got to the outskirts of the village when 2000 Druzes, headed by Selim Bey Jumblatt, were seen rapidly advancing upon it, shouting their war-songs. The Christians, panic-struck, knew not which way to turn. Ere they had time to seize their arms, the avalanche overwhelmed them. The Druzes rushed upon them sword in hand, and cut down every man they met. The women and children fled in dire consternation. With a wild cry of despair the whole population hurried down the nearest ravine, leaving their village behind them already in flames. Twelve hundred men were massacred over the space of two miles, so rapid had been the pursuit. Many took shelter in caves and holes in the rocks, where they remained for days in a state of starvation, not daring to venture out.

A large body took the road to Sidon, being joined on the route by fugitives from other villages similarly attacked. These were waylaid by Kassim Amadi, the confidential agent of Said Bey and his gang, who pursued them to the very gates of Sidon. The Mohammedans of that town refused to let them in. Numbers of the former sallied forth to join the Druzes. The butchery was now consummated; and upwards of 300 bodies soon strewed the sea-beach and the gardens round about. The shrieks of the women and children rent the air. Some were slain; numbers violated. The young girls were hurried off by a mingled horde of Mohammedans and Metualis, who mysteriously appeared and pounced upon them like vultures on their quarry. The Druzes scorned to touch such offal.

Several Catholic convents and nunneries had received letters from Said Bey of exactly similar import on the same day, and were invaded, robbed and pillaged with similar treachery. The nuns were turned out nearly naked into the fields, and in some instances suffered personal violence. The monks who failed in secreting themselves or escaping were pitilessly slaughtered; some speared in derision at the foot of their altars. In the wealthy convent of Meshmousy thirty had their throats cut. The plunder here was something fabulous — in gold vases, cups, jewelled crosses sparkling with diamonds, besides whole heaps of money, the accumulated stores of a century.

The whole was valued at 80,000*l*. The buildings, after being gutted, were burned.

The whole of Said Bey's districts were thus given over to fire and sword; and for a month the work of destruction, rapine and murder was unintermitting. The alarm in Sidon had become appalling. The Moslems hourly vowed death to the Christians; but the opportune arrival of Her Majesty's ship Firefly, commanded by Captain Maunsell, on the 3rd of June, and the vigorous measures taken by that gallant officer, overawed the dark designs of the former, and restored confidence to the latter.

From the very commencement of the hostilities the mob leaders of the Maronites in the Kesrouan, and even bishops, had despatched letters couched in the most inflated and bombastic terms to the great Christian centres amongst the Druzes, calling upon them to rise fearlessly on their oppressors, and promising them immediate assistance. The men of Zachlé, of Deir-el-Kamar, of Jezeen, of Hasbeya, of Rascheya, were told to be of good cheer; this was a war of religion. "The standard of the Cross, blessed by their priests, had been elevated amidst enthusiastic rejoicings. The Maronites had embroidered the Cross on the sleeves of their right arms. They were 50,000 strong, united by one common sentiment, and could afford to distribute their numbers. On a given day 10,000 would march on such a point, 8000 on another, 5000 on another. What had they to fear? Let them rise and strike home. Their cause must be triumphant." The Christians accordingly took heart, daily expected their deliverers, and looked danger boldly in the face. But the promised relief never came, and, in the hour of need, they found themselves left to struggle as best they could.

One of these letters was intercepted by the Druzes; their rage knew no bounds. "This then is a war of religion," said they; "so let it be. The Maronites menace us with destruction; let them come on. But this time, Inshallah! the Druze standards shall be planted on the gates of Tripoli. The country is ours or theirs." The Druzes, in fact, felt it to be a struggle for successful and lasting ascendancy, or irremediable ruin and humiliation. And they declared war to the knife. In their secret councils, they now determined that not a male adult Christian was to be spared. This ever-recurring gangrene of Maronite interference and dictation breaking out in their body politic must be cut out by the roots. All Islamism, if necessary, would rise in their suppo⁊ Then, when the Christian race had been all b⸲⸲ extirpated from among them, and the lands which they had usurped through a long series of years had been restored to their ancient owners, their part of the Lebanon would, as of yore, become the " Mountain of the Druzes."

In the anti-Lebanon, the Druzes, having completed their preparations, began to assume a m⸲ nacing attitude. Sitt Naaify, Said Bey's siste had received from him written instructions. He⸲ word, all over the Wady-el-Tame, which includes Hasbeya and Rascheya, was law. The most venerated ockals bowed to her mandates with implicit obedience. The Shehab emirs ruling in those villages, constantly exposed to the vexatious aggressions of the Druzes on their authority, and even on their properties, not content with seeking the support of the Christians as a counterpoise to the Druzes, had for months and even years, demanded a Turkish garrison, from the pasha of Damascus. The request had been pertinaciously rejected. In the autumn of 1859, to their joy and surprise, their petitions were acceded to; and Osman Bey, with five hundred soldiers, was sent to their support:—a singular concession, most opportunely granted, and exactly calculated to exasperate the Druzes, and rouse all their bitterest passions against the Christians. The Emir Saad-e-deen even accompanied the troops to Hasbeya in person.

When the Christians residing in the villages round about Hasbeya saw the Druzes in that town removing their effects, they were seized with alarm. The elders of Hasbeya sent and invited them to come thither, as a place of security and concentration. The proposal was immediately accepted, and during the last week in May 1860, they and their families, their cattle and their moveables, came pouring in from all directions, most of them being located in the grand quadrangle of the serail. As the danger became more imminent, the Christians raised a subscription of five hundred pounds, which they presented to Osman Bey to insure his fidelity. Women even made him presents of jewellery. He gave them the most solemn assurances of his friendship and support, and they became somewhat tranquillised.

Early on Sunday, June 3rd, the Druze forces were seen crowning all the heights overhanging Hasbeya. For days previously Osman Bey had constantly been at the house of Sitt Naaify, where a few of his soldiers were always stationed. In fact, nothing could be done without reference to Sitt Naaify. Said Bey had already come in person from Mu*ch*tara and had an interview with Osman Bey and the Turkish aga commanding at Rascheya, at a spring between those two places. The Christians on seeing the Druzes, implored Osman Bey to act: he affected to parley with them, sent an officer to know their intentions, who returned with the answer that they were about to attack. He then told the Christians to go out and defend themselves, and he would in case of necessity support them.

A few hundreds advanced and took up a widely extended position, thinking thus to cover the entire circumference of the town; — a disorderly crowd of beardless youths and lads, without orders or even a leader. The leaders, those who should have been at their head, to give directions, remained idly in the serail, clinging to their protectors, the Turks. Shots were exchanged for about half an hour, when the Druzes making directly on a given point *en masse*, carried everything before them. The discomfited Christians now rushed bodily to the serail and were admitted. Osman Bey, to have an appearance of making good his word, pointed his cannon and fired two rounds of canister indiscriminately. Several of the retreating Christians and two or three of the advancing Druzes were knocked over. The Druzes now spread over the town, and in the course of two hours it was all wrapt in flames.

Osman Bey then went up to Sitt Naaify and asked her wishes. She demanded an unconditional surrender on the part of the Christians and the delivering up of their arms. With her consent, Osman Bey gave them a written guarantee, pledging the faith of the government for their personal safety. The following morning she came together with Osman Bey to the serail. The helpless Christians consented perforce to the mournful arrangement. Their arms were all heaped together in the middle of the grand court. The best among them were selected by the Druzes and Turks. The remainder, about eight hundred stand, were packed on mules and consigned to Druze carriers, ostensibly to be taken to Damascus. These likewise, however, were afterwards taken by the Druzes.

The Turkish aga at Rascheya, immediately after his interview with Said Bey, had placed a cordon of soldiers all round that town, to prevent all possible egress by the Christians. Many tried to escape to Hasbeya, but were repulsed by them. On the morning of the 4th of June, the Turkish soldiers fired a signal. The town was shortly afterwards attacked by 1500 Druzes. In the same way as at Jezeen and other places, the Christians had just been assured of the peaceable intentions of their enemies. All had dispersed to their usual labours with a perfect feeling of security. Thus taken by surprise, they had barely time to seize their arms and rush to their houses. But once there, they maintained a resolute defence the whole day, inflicting a deadly loss on their numerous assailants. As the shades of night closed round them, having expended all their ammunition, they abandoned their barricades and thronged to the serail, whither the Shehab emirs had preceded them. Their friends, the Turks, received them with open arms, invited them all in, closed the gates upon them, and swore to defend them at the hazard of their lives.

In the mean time the unfortunate Christians in the serail at Hasbeya, were enduring the double misery of imprisonment and starvation. Water was hardly to be got. Bread was still scarcer, and what little they got was at exorbitant prices. Their ordinary food was bran, dried beans and vine leaves. The women, in despair, tore off all their trinkets, and gave them to the Turkish soldiers, to move them to pity. All now looked to Sitt Naaify as their sole deliverer. Wives and daughters went up to her house, pushed madly into her presence, threw themselves at her feet, and in passionate accents of grief implored an order for the release of their husbands and fathers. She was as cold and hard as marble. Some there were, however, who had come in from the neighbouring country, tenants on the lands belonging to her son-in-law, Selim Bey. These were taken out and brought to her. Were they to be killed, those lands would rest without cultivators. Besides, she argued, by giving shelter and protection to a few, she might triumphantly point to them, in case of a day of account ever coming, as proofs that she had mercifully and successfully interceded on behalf of the Christians.

News of these proceedings had already reached Damascus. The heads of the Greek Church, the bishops, the clergy, and the European consuls had all gone in a body to Achmed Pasha and demanded his prompt intervention and assistance. They were met at first by expressions of regret at the weakness of the military force at his disposal; then he would send orders to Mustapha Pasha, who was in the Houran, to despatch, if possible, a regiment to Hasbeya; then Mustapha Pasha could not weaken his division, every man of whom was wanted, to enable him to restrain the insurgent Arabs. Wearied with such excuses and prevarications, the consuls begged an order, merely an order, to Osman Bey to bring all the Christians of Hasbeya and Rascheya to Damascus. The pasha could not well back out of this, and the order was made out.

It was taken by his own aide-de-camp in person to Kenj-il-Amad,—a Druze sheik in the employ of the government, who was entrusted with the police force stationed to preserve order in the Bekaa,— with instructions for him to proceed forthwith to Hasbeya and see the order executed. This zealous and efficient public officer, who, singularly enough, was only appointed to his command by Achmed Pasha, two months previously, had been employing the last fortnight in laying waste the whole of the Bekaa with fire and sword; burning down all the Christian villages, and slaying every Christian he could overtake. On the receipt of the order, he proceeded with the aide-de-camp to the village of Karaoon, near the Wady-el-Tame, assembled the Christians there, congratulated them on their approaching safety, and at the head of 150 horse, took them on with him to Hasbeya.

On his road he was joined by Ali Bey Hamadi, the Lieutenant of Said Bey Jumblatt. He had been summoned to Muchtara, had received his instructions, and was now on his way to Hasbeya, with a reinforcement of 300 men. They reached the environs about mid-day on the 10th of June, the sound of their kettledrums reverberating through the valley. The arms and banners of the victorious Druzes were shining and fluttering under the rays of a glorious sun, over the blackened and deserted town. They arrived at the serail and dismounted. On entering, they thrust in the fugitives from Karaoon, and then gave Achmed Pasha's order to Osman Bey, who read it aloud. The Christians knew no bounds to their joy. At last the hour of deliverance had come. Cries of "Long live the Sultan,—long live our gracious protectors," burst from every lip. They threw themselves wildly into each other's arms, and mutual kisses were frantically exchanged. All began to pick up the few articles of clothing they had left. The more emaciated ventured to ask for animals to carry them. Surely they would not be left to perish on the way. They only wanted them for one day. To-morrow they would all be at Damascus!

The two Druze chiefs then went to pay their

respects to Sitt Naaify, and were cordially received. Time was pressing, and they had a mission to perform. All depended upon Sitt Naaify. Whatever was to be said, must be said quickly. Ali Hamadi had to make a last, perhaps a presumptuous appeal, and he made it. Said Bey was inflexible, but a woman's heart might yet relent. "Are the Christians all to be massacred?" said he, earnestly looking in her face. "Think of their families, the widows and the orphan babes, and take compassion. Spare those fine young men, those beardless lads. Execute the leaders, the most turbulent, the most obnoxious. Come down and see them executed with your own eyes, if you will; but spare, oh, spare the rest!" "Impossible!" she exclaimed, "impossible; my brother's orders are peremptory and explicit," holding a letter from him in her hands; "not a Christian is to be left alive from seven to seventy years." Not another syllable was uttered, and the chiefs descended to the serail, whither the Druzes had already thronged, tumultuously.

The mask was now thrown off. Osman Bey ordered the trumpets to sound. The soldiers stood to their arms. The serail is three stories high, with spacious chambers and lofty corridors. Many of the Christians were scattered throughout them, joyfully preparing for their departure. The soldiers were ordered to go up and drive them into the great central court. With savage joy, the Turks ran up and searched every nook and corner for the poor wretches, and then forced them down at the bayonet's point, insulting, beating, stabbing them, and plucking the clothes off their backs as they reeled along. The women and children followed in wild agony, screaming and imploring, and even yet hoping to interpose and save.

The gates of the serail were thrown open, the Druzes rushed in with a loud yell. But there was yet to be a pause. The soldiers were still mingled more or less with the crowd. Time was to be given them to get away. After a few minutes the arena was declared to be ready. The Turks had all mounted, some to the corridors, some to the terraces, where they ranged themselves like spectators at a theatre, expecting a grand spectacle. And now the butchery began.

The Druzes, from their standing place, first fired a general volley, and then sprung on the Christians with yatagans, hatchets and bill-hooks.

The first victim was Yoosuf Reis, the confidential secretary of the Emir Saad-e-deen. He clung to the knees of Osman Bey. Osman Bey, to whom he had paid two hundred pounds in hard money, to be protected. The ruffian kicked him with his foot on the mouth, and sent him staggering. He was seized and cut up piece-meal, beginning with his fingers and toes. The Emir Saad-e-deen was next decapitated, and his head sent as a trophy to Said Bey forthwith. By degrees the moving mass was hewn into. Many had their noses, ears and lips cut off, and were otherwise horribly mutilated, before the final blow was given. The women pressed back to the walls all round, filled the air with their shrieks. If any tried to save a beloved one, she was cut down. Yet many a mother might be seen bending down and cowering over her boy, hugging him to her bosom, trying to conceal him beneath her robes, and when discovered, winding around him a frenzied clasp, and struggling as only mothers can. The sword alone could dissever that fond embrace, and loosen that convulsive hold; and mother and child alike expired beneath the fatal gash — their blood commingling.

A few Christians, at first, tried to escape by the gate. The Turkish soldiers seized them, stripped their clothes off them, and delivered them over to the Druzes; in more than one instance indeed despatching them themselves. As the slaughter went on the galleries resounded with fierce acclamations. "Give him a slash for the French." "Another for his consul." "God strengthen your hands." Such were the ejaculatory cries which thence proceeded. But from the martyr throng, scarcely a groan, and not even a prayer for mercy arose. Each one, as his turn came, calmly submitted his body to the stroke, gently begged not to be tortured, and ever and anon fervently muttered,— " In Thy name Lord Jesus." And his murderer responded, "Eh! call upon your Jesus, and see whether he can help you now! Don't you know God is a Druze!"

Sitt Naaify came down and entered the serail about an hour after sunset. It was dark. She called for a lamp. It was brought her. Ordering it to be held up before her, she for a long time feasted her eyes on the ghastly sight. Several hundred mangled corpses lay heaped up over each other before her. "Well done my good and faithful Druzes," she exclaimed; "this is just what I expected from you." The women and some of the Shehab emirs who had been hidden in their own harem, now thronged around her. The latter kissed her feet and implored for pardon and forgiveness. She told them all to follow her. The Turks were all this time seen flitting about like spectres through the court, under cover of the darkness, turning over the dead bodies, if perchance they might grope up some plunder; and wherever life yet lingered, giving the "coup de grâce."

CHAP. VI.

June 11, 1860, the Massacre at Kanakin by Ismail-il-Uttrush. — The Christians hunted down like wild Beasts. — June 14, Zach*l*é invested and taken. — June 19, Deir-el-Kamar entered by the Druzes; ruthless Slaughter of the entire male Population. — Deir-el-Kamar in flames. — The surviving Widows and Children fly to the Coast. — June 22, Disturbances at Beyrout. — General Kmety (Ismail Pasha). — The purely Maronite Districts in danger. — The European Consuls-General admonish the Druzes. — Mr. Graham's Mission to Said Bey Jumblatt and the Druze Sheiks.

ISMAIL-IL-UTTRUSH and his Druzes, amounting to 3000 men, of whom one half were horse, were in movement within four and twenty hours from the receipt of the letter spoken of in the last chapter from Said Bey Jumblatt. They made direct for the Wady-el-Tame, which they reached on the third day. On their second day's march they arrived at Kanakin, a large Mohammedan village, ten hours from Hasbeya. Numerous

Christians who were employed getting in the harvest round about had fled thither, hoping for protection. Eager to flesh their swords, the Druzes slew them to a man. On the 11th of June, they passed under the heights of Rascheya, intending to push on for Zachlé. Being summoned however by loud shouts, to ascend to the former village, they turned aside, went up and halted in front of the serail. There, for some days past, the Turks had been amusing themselves by stripping and robbing of everything they possessed those unfortunate Christians, 150 in number, who had lately looked to them with implicit confidence as their saviours. Their victims were now ready for slaughter.

Ismail-il-Uttrush held a conference apart with the Turkish aga. In the twinkling of an eye the gates of the serail were thrown open, and the Druzes rushed in. What followed was an exact epitome of all that had happened at Hasbeya the day before. The Shehab emirs, though Mohammedans, were all massacred: their mortal sin was that they had befriended the Christians. This bloody interlude over, the Druzes of the Houran and of the Wady-el-Tame joined their forces, making altogether about 5000 men, and pushed on to the Bekaa. At the same time, the Turkish garrisons of Hasbeya and Rascheya repaired to Damascus, where, for weeks afterwards, they openly sold their plunder in the public bazaars: watches, jewellery, shawls, church vessels and richly embroidered priestly robes.

The sight which greeted Ismail-il-Uttrush and his hordes, on emerging into the Bekaa, elated their hopes and whetted their thirst for vengeance. Dark volumes of smoke arose on every side from burnt and ransacked villages. Occasionally parties of terrified Christian fugitives would cross their path, hurrying on to gain the nearest mountain recesses, coverts in the bush, or caves in the rock. The men were immolated on the spot;— the women plundered and allowed to proceed. Even the distant plain of Baalbec sent forth athwart the skies its flaming tokens of disaster and horror.

There, also, the Christians were being hunted down like wild beasts, their houses fired, their men slain, their women violated; for the Turk presided over the orgies. The fierce Metualis vied with each other in the pitiless cruelty of their onslaughts, while the Turkish officer in command, at the head of his irregulars, ever led the way, and shone conspicuous in the van. Even from the mosques and minarets the shout for blood arose; and, mingled with the muezzin's call to prayer, might be heard a cry informing the faithful that by an imperial firman the Christions were devoted to destruction, and their lives and properties had become a lawful prey.

The civil war had now been raging in the Lebanon for three weeks, in every direction, to the complete discomfiture of the Christians living amongst the Druzes. The Maronite emirs and sheiks, who ought and might have advanced to their assistance, never once crossed the frontier which divided them from the Druzes. The 50,000 warriors so loudly vaunted remained in a state of shameful inaction. Thousands would assemble on a given point within their own territory, waste away several days in consuming the rations they had brought with them, beg for more in 'the village in which they quartered themselves, then gradually dwindle away, and finally disappear.

The Christian kaimmakam, already sold to the Turks, had prevailed on the emir belonging to his family to take no part in the contest, and without them their followers and adherents would not move. Most of the former secretly wished success to the Druzes. The democratic tendencies, which had proved so fatal to the feudal power of the Haazin sheiks in the Kesrouan, might yet prove fatal to their own. Already their peasants had shown signs of sympathy, if not of revolt. The triumph of the Druzes was that of feudalism. On more than one occasion, indeed, the Druzes had offered their services to support the feudal rights of the Maronite emirs, if menaced by insurgency.

The deadly enemies of the Druzes were not the Maronite aristocracy, but the Maronite clergy. The former never embarked heartily in any movement against them. The Shehab emirs, with no feudal retainers whatever, and important only by the prestige of their name, were, whenever they appeared on the scene, merely the tools of the latter, and drew upon themselves accordingly a large share of Druze rancour and hatred. None of the Maronite sheiks from the north stirred at all. One, indeed, advanced with large pretensions, a large force, and still larger menaces, and at last pleaded consular prohibition as an excuse for his cowardly inefficiency. Under all these circumstances, it cannot be surprising that the Druzes swept the field.

Everything now seemed to augur for them a victorious ascendancy, such as they had never yet achieved, and could indeed have hardly contemplated. But two strongholds yet remained to the Christians, Deir-el-Kamar and Zach/lé; the one indeed humbled, but the other proud and defiant as ever. Could their standards once be planted there, the Christians in the mountains of the Druzes would henceforth be their serfs and slaves. All their energies were now about to be concentrated on Zach/lé. From every part the Druze forces gathered around that devoted town. Ismail-il-Uttrush encamped within two miles of the place, and was immediately joined by large parties of Arabs and Kurds, attracted to the spot like vultures by the smell of carrion. The Metualis from Baalbec, under the emirs of the house of Harfoosh, had likewise promised a large contingent.

The leading Christians of Zach̀lé, seeing the storm thus about to burst over them, wrote in pathetic terms to the European consuls-general, imploring their prompt interference with Kurchid Pasha, in order that a military force might be sent to protect them. A Turkish regiment was consequently ordered to march thither; but in place of entering the town, it halted at two hours distance from it, and in such a position as to enable it, in case of need, to co-operate with the Druzes. The commandant, shortly after his arrival, sent for the principal Druze sheiks, and remained in friendly conference with them all the night. Early the next morning the Druze chiefs returned to their posts in high spirits, and no doubt well assured by the courteous demeanour and effective sympathy of their cordial allies, the Turks.*

The people of Zach̀lé were now busily engaged

---

* Papers relating to disturbances in Syria, p. 35.

in taking measures for a desperate defence. In their own idea the town was impregnable. They encouraged each other by calling to mind how, in the year 1841, the Druze forces broke upon it like waves upon a rock, to be scattered like the spray; how on that occasion their church bells miraculously tolled, the Virgin Mary herself clearly interposing in their behalf. And then, with a blasphemy singularly contrasting with such abject superstition, they fired their muskets upwards in the broad face of heaven, shouting that "God himself could not take Zachlé!"

Such was the insolent turbulence of the Christians in Zachlé, that they had long rejected the authority of their kaimmakams, had risen in rebellion against their own emirs, refusing them their legal dues; had appointed a municipality of their own; and, as is generally the case where a commonalty breaks the bonds of restraint, they were all the while divided into factions seeking each other's blood, sometimes actually shedding it, and scarcely to be reconciled even before the impending crisis.

They had, as their towns enlarged and their numbers increased, obtained augmented reputation and increased prestige. Zachlé was the shield of the Christians, the terror of the Druzes. Certainly, within a certain radius from its habitations, no Christian, no matter whence he came, could ever be insulted with impunity. The Druzes looked upon it with misgiving. It was not lightly to be touched. But now the tide of war came surging on, and its metal was to undergo the decisive test. On learning the near approach of the Druzes, its leaders had assembled together, appointed chiefs, and assigned posts. But orders cheerfully received one moment were disobeyed the next. The enthusiasm of the morning vanished amidst jealous disputes before the evening. Accusations of treason or foolhardiness were mutually retorted. But the cloud was rapidly gathering; the enemy were at their gates. It was necessary to do something.

On the 14th of June a body of 200 horse and 600 foot sallied forth into the plain of the Bakaa to meet their foe. At an hour's distance they were in sight. The Christians, heedless of discipline and blindly regardless of danger, spread themselves over the fields, some standing up, others lining ditches, and commenced an indiscriminate firing. The Druze infantry came on to the encounter in compact masses, and returned the fusillade, leaving it to their cavalry to carry the day. The latter, joined by a tumultuous band of Kurds and Arabs, careered wildly about, and soon enveloped the straggling Christians on every side, picking them off one by one. Their flight soon became general. The Christian horse were ridden over and dispersed. The Arabs and Druzes returned to their camp, carrying seventy Christian heads on the points of their spears. On the following day the Christians made another sortie on a larger scale, but with similar results. They now confined themselves to self-defence.

Adjoining to Zachlé, indeed so close as to merit being called a suburb, is the small village of Malaka, the residence of the Turkish kaimmakam of the Bekaa, and the quarters of a small Turkish garrison. These had of course been instructed to play their part. The Christians here, as elsewhere, had constantly confided their fears and apprehensions to the Turkish officers near them, and in like manner received the most flattering assurances of their good-will and sympathy. They were the Sultan's subjects, and the imperial troops were bound to protect them. An officer arrived on the 16th at Malaka, charged with a mission from Kurchid Pasha, to inquire into the state of the Christians at Zachlé, with a view to rendering them every succour and assistance they might require. The Christians, now in the depth of their emergency, received him with joy and gratitude, and earnestly begged for more troops. He left the following morning with promises of speedy reinforcements.

On his way back to Beyrout, he met bands of Druzes, from time to time, singing their war songs and hurrying towards the scene of action. "Forward, forward to Zachlé," he would say, pointing in that direction, "to-morrow I will be with you." After an hour's interview with Kurchid Pasha he returned, according to his word, with more soldiers, but not to Zachlé. The Christians in that now beleaguered town were in the mean time daily importuned by the Turkish kaimmakam to give up their arms and confide entirely in him and the Turkish troops, now so near at hand.

By so doing, it was represented to them, they would assume a peaceful attitude, give an unquestionable token of their friendly intentions, and throw the onus and responsibility of the war on the Druzes. If, after that, the latter dared to attack, the imperial troops would resist them to the death.

Many began to incline to these plausible propositions, by which their own blood might be spared, and the general security ensured, but the majority decided that it was better to trust to their own right arms, and to die for their honour and their faith; or that, in the case of irremediable defeat, the mountains were at their backs, to which they could as a last resort retire with their families. Fortunate indeed was such a decision. Their good star prevailed. Had they surrendered their arms and remained, they would have been massacred to a man.

On the morning of the 18th, the Druzes attacked with tactical skill and decision. For four hours they poured in a continuous fire from the gardens stretching along the foot of the town. The Christians concentrated all their strength in that direction, and fought with great bravery. Their whole force amounted to about 4000 men. The Druzes and their allies mustered nearly double that number. Suddenly from the heights above a body of 1200 Druzes were seen steadily descending. Disdaining to reply to the feeble volleys which saluted them, they marched on, sword in hand. Numbers of them fell, but nothing could check their onward movement. In less than half an hour the band was in the centre of the town. While some engaged in a hand-to-hand struggle with the Christians in the streets, others set fire to the houses. The flames spread rapidly, and soon the conflagration became general. The Christians, panic struck, abandoned all their positions, and took to flight.

And now amidst the din of battle, the voice of Druze criers was distinctly heard: "Spare the women! Spare the women! by orders of our chief, Hottar Amad: whoever touches a woman shall be shot!" A Druze escort was rapidly organised to conduct them safely out of reach of danger. Every male, however, who was overtaken, of whatever age, except infants, was pitilessly slain. The main body of the Turkish troops pressed close on the Druzes as they broke in from the gardens, while many of the soldiers mingled in their ranks and joined in their fire. The whole remaining population of Zachlé gained the mountains to the north ere sunset, and were soon in the Maronite districts, whither the Druzes cared not for the present to pursue them.

The news of the taking of Zachlé spread like wild-fire through the Lebanon. Received by the Druzes with exuberant and even frantic rejoicings, and by the Christians with dismay and consternation; all felt the struggle was now over. Bloody episodes might yet occur, but the Christian cause was lost. Lost shamefully, ignominiously. Turkish treachery and Maronite cowardice had consummated its ruin. Though 15,000 Maronites were standing by their arms within six hours of Zachlé, not one moved to its defence. During the short but eventful contest they never once ventured to cross over into the Druze districts, to the relief of their co-religionists. The latter were essentially the victims of the hollow professions of the Maronites, and miserably expiated with their blood the treason of their selfish aristocracy, and the bombastic ravings of their bigoted and contemptible priesthood.

Zach́lé had fallen: but while Deir-el-Kamar stood, the Druze triumph was yet, in their eyes, incomplete, and on it the Druzes now rushed like ravenous wolves. It was true it had surrendered, but the dictates of an all-absorbing vengeance knew no laws, human or divine.

Detached parties of Druzes commenced entering that town on the 19th. Wherever they met the Christians they disarmed them. They next proceeded to enter and pillage the shops and houses. In the afternoon some Turkish soldiers fired a volley. Immediately the sound of the Druze musketry was heard on all sides. The Christians fled in consternation to the serail and asked the kaimmakam what all this meant. "Had he not sworn to resist any attack which the Druzes might make on them? Already they were pouring into the town by hundreds and thousands." They were told, in reply, that there was no real cause for alarm, but for greater security they had better bring all their valuables to the serail, where they would remain untouched until order was restored. Forthwith men, women and children, began streaming into that building from every quarter, carrying trunks, chests and bundles filled with clothes, linen and jewellery, with gold, pearls and diamonds in profusion: an immense booty, which the Turks proceeded to divide amongst themselves.

The slaughter next commenced. Whenever a Christian was seen, he was shot or cut down. Flames at the same time burst forth in various places. Dark volumes of smoke hung brooding over the town. The shouting, swearing and screaming was appalling. The priests fled to their churches, and were slain at the foot of the altars. All who followed them to the sacred edifices were butchered on the pavement. The Turkish soldiers ran about calling on the Druzes to come out of the houses where they were pillaging, and to think only of killing the giaours. They would stand guard over the plunder until the work was done.

On the morning of the 20th, the Druzes, headed by Ali Bey Hamadi, congregated in front of the serail, which now contained upwards of 1200 fugitives, with their families. The kaimmakam refused to open the gates, but pointed to a low wall close by. Instantly the Druzes began clambering over and pouring into the grand court, like bloodhounds into a sheepfold.

The women were ordered to separate from the men and fall back. For some time husbands clung to their wives, sons to their mothers, but the flashing sword soon effected the fatal separation. All the horrors of Hasbeya were now renewed. The blows given by hatchets, axes and bill-hooks, as they fell on the human body, sounded like those of woodcutters felling a forest. Every kind of blasphemy, imprecation, and insult, which heart could devise or tongue pronounce, was vented by the Druzes on their helpless victims. Did any try to conceal themselves, they were hunted out and dragged forth by the Turks. Did a Druze perchance show mercy, the Turk was there to taunt him with his weakness and urge him to complete the deed.

For six long hours the infernal work went on. The blood at length rose above the ankles, flowed along the gutters, gushed out of the water spouts, and gurgled through the streets. Standing on their ghastly and mutilated prey, the Druzes now turned to the women, and, with swords at their breasts, told them to shout, "Long live our victorious lord, Ali Hamadi;" and the poor trembling creatures, with tears running down their cheeks, their voices choked with sobs, their hair dishevelled, and the skirts of their gowns dabbling in blood, cried out, "Long live our victorious lord, Ali Hamadi." The Turkish colonel all the while sat at the gate smoking his pipe, the bowl resting on a corpse.

The Druze sheiks had planned this atrocious butchery at Deir-el-Kamar, from the time it surrendered. Said Bey Jumblatt in the course of the three weeks following that event had ridden daily over from Mu*ch*tara and held close conclave with his colleagues and the Turkish kaimmakam in the palace of Beit-e-deen, which overlooks the town. His Kehié, Ali Hamadi, on leaving these conferences, constantly terrified the Christians by telling them it had been decided not to leave a male of them alive. A few respectable Christians had fled to Mu*ch*tara at the commencement of hostilities, trusting to their former friendship with Said Bey. They had been well received. But when they asked, on their knees, to be allowed to send for their relatives, the request had always been denied as impracticable. The latter were not wanted, the former might be turned to good account. Accordingly, as the sanguinary climax approached, they were sent for into the Bey's presence, and forced to fix their signatures and seals to a document purporting that he had uniformly treated the Christians with the greatest kindness and humanity, and had done all he could to save them. The next day three Christians had their heads struck off in front of his divan.

On the morning of the massacre Said Bey judged it politic to be absent both from Muchtara and Deir-el-Kamar. At either place he might have been appealed to by the terror-stricken Christians to stay the horrors. Had he refused to interfere it might hereafter prove a damning fact against him. He provided himself an excellent means of escape from such a dilemma. Shortly after sunrise he left Muchtara at the head of a half-clad, miserable band of Christians, composed of men, women and children, giving out that he meant to take them in person to Sidon. "How nobly," it would be said, "he protected the Christians, actually escorting them himself!" He went no further however than Djoun. There he abandoned his mission of mercy. Things of mightier import weighed upon his mind.

Speeding back to Deir-el-Kamar, as with an eagle's flight, he alighted in the grand square in front of the serail shortly after dusk. The town was all in flames. Columns of fire shot up and boomed to and fro with scorching blasts. Houses every moment fell in with hideous crash. Demoniac yells and piercing shrieks rent the air. The earth emitted a gory steam. Mangled bodies lay scattered about in mounds, some yet palpitating. Joining his lieutenant, Ali Hamadi, he walked up and down for a short time, made a few jesting remarks, eyed the huge writhing carcase with furtive glance, and suddenly disappeared.

Early in the afternoon Kurchid Pasha had arrived from Beyrout. Passing through the town he went direct to Beit-e-deen. Within its walls more than one hundred Christians had just perished at the hands of the Turkish soldiers and Druzes: for twenty-four hours after his arrival the massacres continued in various places without intermission. In dark vaults, in sewers, in every possible hiding-place, the relentless sword pursued and smote its victims. Some were taken out and crucified, some were burnt alive. At last the pasha fired a signal gun, and the carnage forthwith ceased. The Druze sheiks joyous and exulting now went to pay him their respects. They were cordially received. The Turks and Druzes had gained a joint victory.

The next day a mournful crowd of nearly two thousand widows and orphan children assembled outside their once happy abode, wringing their hands with wild despair. Emaciated with hunger, fever-stricken with long and painful watching and excitement, almost senseless with excessive weeping, scarcely covered with decent clothing, their desolation was complete. The Abou Nakad sheiks came and ordered them to move on. Under their charge, the long mournful train descended into the ravine, and took the road to the sea-side. The same evening they reached the banks of the Damoor, between Beyrout and Sidon. The Druze chiefs now addressed a letter to the English consul-general, informing him of their arrival at that spot with the female survivors from Deir-el-Kamar, and requesting him to send boats to convey them away. Singular application! as though they thought that all the atrocities they had committed would be taken as a matter of course, and that England would sympathetically relieve them of their present embarrassment.

Her Majesty's ships, Gannet and Mohawk were immediately ordered to effect the embarcation of the wretched fugitives. No sooner had their boats come within sight than a general rush was made to the beach. The women threw themselves frantically into the foaming surge, some holding their infants high above their heads. Several had received sabre cuts. Most of them had not tasted food for four days. All vented their imprecations against the Turks rather than Druzes. "The Turks have murdered us!" they cried "the Turks have murdered us!" Not only at the mouth of the Damoor, but all along the coasts of Tyre and Sidon, crowds of bereaved sufferers, flying from all parts of the mountain, were seen wending their weary way. The two latter cities were thronged with hundreds, exposed night and day to the taunts, derision and menaces of an excited Mohammedan population. By the unintermitting exertions of Commanders West and Lambert and their efficient crews, all were finally rescued and brought round to Beyrout, which itself in the mean time had undergone a serious crisis.

On the 22nd of June a Mohammedan was assassinated close to the walls of that city. Immediately the shout arose that a Christian had committed the deed. All the shops were at once deserted. An armed rabble paraded the streets crying aloud for vengeance, and declaring the time had come. A panic seized the Christians, who crowded round the various consulates and took shelter in European houses. The court of justice was surrounded by the Moslem mob, who arrogantly threatened the authorities that if the murderer was not executed by sunset they would rise on the Christians during the night and massacre them. The danger was imminent. Even Europeans passing through the streets were insulted. The French consul-general had a sword flourished in his face. An Englishman had a pistol snapped at him.

At this critical juncture a Turkish line-of-battle ship anchored in the port with troops under the command of Ismail Pasha (General Kmety), who were instantly disembarked. The nerve and coolness displayed by that gallant officer somewhat reassured the Christians. He offered, if necessary, to bombarb the town. Captain Paynter, of the Exmouth, had, with equal promptness, offered to land all his available force. Still the Moslems vociferously demanded a reprisal. An unfortunate young Christian, seen near the spot where the murdered man had fallen, had been seized. He was dragged along and nearly torn to pieces. The mockery of a trial was forthwith commenced. Conviction and sentence of death of course followed. The poor lad calmly and heroically said, "I am innocent, God knows I am innocent; but if my death is necessary for the safety of my brethren, I gladly give up my life:" and he was taken beyond the gate and executed.

Thus, the expiatory sacrifice was accomplished, and tranquillity restored.

This effect on the public mind was however merely momentary. Fear and agitation pervaded all classes. Every hour brought in news of intended movements on the part of the Druzes. Tyre was menaced. Sidon was about to be attacked. And again English and French ships of war were started off at a moment's notice to give protection to all the threatened points. The state of Beyrout itself became daily more and more lamentable. Druzes armed up to the teeth continually entered the town, walked with braggart air through the bazaars, received the embraces and congratulations of the Mohammedans, and left with their firearms decked with flowers and garlands. Commerce was completely paralysed. The Ottoman bank shipped all its bullion. English merchant-steamers laden with goods were ordered to take their cargoes back to Malta. The principal native Christian families, and even the tradespeople and lower orders, left daily by thousands, in any ships they could obtain, for Alexandria, Scyra and Athens. Boats were stationed ready to take off the European residents at a moment's notice. Nothing could convince the Christian population of Beyrout, but that the fate of their brethren at Deir-el-Kamar, Hasbeya and Rascheya, awaited them, at the hands of the Turks, their authorities and their troops.*

The attitude now assumed by the Druzes had excited the liveliest inquietude for the fate of the purely Maronite districts of the Lebanon. They had not as yet crossed the Dog river, but they already talked of an invasion in that direction as a necessary climax to their amazing triumph. More fatal sign than any, Kurchid Pasha had issued orders to two Turkish regiments to hold themselves in readiness to march into the Kesrouan *to protect the Maronites !* From the moment this ominous fact became known, the European consuls-general felt there was not another moment to be lost. They had seen the nature of that *protection,* and it required no great clearness of prophetic vision to foresee that its extension to the Maronite districts, containing some thousand

---

* Papers relating to disturbances in Syria, p. 48.

villages and nearly half a million of souls, was simply equivalent to handing them over to a combined attack of Turks and Druzes, and their consequent devastation by fire and sword.

Mr. Moore, her Majesty's consul-general, in consequence, assembled his colleagues on the 27th of June, and suggested the experiment of addressing a collective note directly to the Druze chiefs themselves. By addressing Kurchid Pasha they would only get deeper into the mire. How often had they done so, only to be ridiculed and deceived. Besides, Kurchid Pasha was now at Sidon, superintending, as it were, the Druze atrocities, which were being daily committed under his very eyes, in that neighbourhood, without any steps whatever being taken to curb the perpetrators.* If the Turk was insatiable of Christian blood, the Druze might yet perchance be amenable to reason. The alliance between the two would thus be adroitly dissevered. The massacres might then cease.

The following representation was accordingly drawn up. "It is with the greatest regret that

* Further papers relating to disturbances in Syria, p. 20.

we, the consuls-general of England, Austria, France, Prussia and Russia, are obliged to state that pillage, massacres and devastation, continue in such a measure as to merit our highest disapprobation. We charge you then formally to put an immediate stop to all these disasters; and as the representatives of the Great Powers, and in the names of our embassies, which have given us formal instructions on this head, we warn you that a heavy responsibility will rest upon you for the future, if any further movements are directed by you or your people against the Christians, their villages, or their property. To arrive at this object, it is urgent, and we charge you most energetically, to make peace with as little delay as possible, and to recall such of your bands as may be found in the direction of Damascus, Sidon, Zacḥlé, Deir-el-Kamar, and the Kesrouan, or any other locality. Reflect on the disastrous consequences which may arise to all on non-compliance with the demands we now make to you; and consider that our governments cannot look with indifference on the continuation of such a state of things."

This document was entrusted to Mr. Graham, an English traveller, who started with it the same day to Muchtara, the residence of Said Bey Jumblatt, where he arrived early the following morning.

The *English subject*, as he audaciously styled himself, received his visitor with constrained courtesy and conscience-stricken embarrassment: and hurriedly ascertaining the purport of his mission, mounted his horse, rode off, and unceremoniously left him in the lurch. He did not return till after dark, when he condescended to apply himself to the subject matter in hand. After having listened to all the requests made, all the arguments and expostulations adduced by his guest, he unburdened his mind at intervals, in nearly the following terms: " Me send for the sheiks, why there would not be the slightest good in my sending for them; they would not come at my calling. As for writing to them, that would be ridiculous. I have no power whatever over them; indeed, we are on bad terms with each other. I should be glad to allow some of my horsemen to accompany you, if you wish to go round and visit the sheiks; but not one of them will stir an inch. To-morrow is a feast day.

"I have never interfered in any way whatever in the war. I have always done all I possibly could for the Christians. My constant endeavours have been to pacify and keep down the Druzes; but they wont listen to me. I have no power over my people. The commonest man among them disobeys my orders and laughs at my authority. I know all sorts of absurd reports have been spread about my being an influential person amongst the Druzes, and all the blame of what is happening has been laid most unjustly at my door. As for making any promises of peace, that is entirely out of the question. I have always been, in my humble sphere, a great admirer, and, indeed, a great friend of the English, and I should be sorry to think that I could ever do anything to forfeit the confidence of the British government. However, it may do what it likes. I am the Queen's devoted slave : let her do as she pleases."

Another "English subject" was present at the delivery of these ejaculatory remarks, and strongly vouched for its truth and correctness, pleading at the same time his own ignorance and innocence of all that had been going on—no less a magnate than Beshir Bey Abou Nakad, who had formerly sworn that he would lay the foundation of his house near Deir-el-Kamar with Christian skulls, and who now of course was perfectly able to do so whenever he chose.

Mr. Graham, nothing daunted by the withering derision to which he had thus been exposed, and finding, to his great surprise, that these two beys were mere nonentities, determined to try his luck with other Druze sheiks who might confess to being somebodies, and made his round accordingly. No fox-hunter was ever more puzzled or perplexed. Most of the foxes got wind of him. Some ran to earth and were never more heard of. Others dodged, but were finally overtaken, only to give proof of their subtlety and cunning. "The English of the East," in fact, were all much of the same type. Mr. Graham, however, saw and heard sufficient to convince him that something was planning, and wrote to the English consul-general that Beyrout and Sidon had better keep a sharp lookout. The mission had thus apparently proved a failure. Nevertheless, the Druze chiefs, however wary in their language and tenacious of their dignity, which would have been sorely compromised by appearing to yield to dictation, were far too astute to persevere in their intended policy, when thus powerfully contravened; and from this moment they never made a forward or even an aggressive movement. The English consul-general's calculations were correct, his interposition well timed; and the Lebanon reposed.

The Turks, having now attained their object by a sweeping massacre of the Christians in the Druze districts, thought the sooner affairs were patched up the better. Kurchid Pasha proposed that peace should be proclaimed between the two sects, on the condition that the past should be forgotten, no plunder restored, and no indemnification given. The Maronite emirs and sheiks were summoned to Beyrout to give their consent and co-operation to this arrangement. Remonstrance and complaint on their part were alike vain. If they yielded, the sword might be suspended; if not, it had yet good work to do, and would be allowed to do it. To the intense satisfaction of the Druzes, the Christian chiefs put their seals to a treaty consecrating these principles. Their ascendancy, with undisturbed possession of power, was now established for ever. Maronite interference with the few Christian slaves who remained under them, would never again be attempted; and the properties of the massacred would naturally revert to them as lords of the soil.

CHAP. VII.

July 9, 1860, the Mohammedans of Damascus rise upon the Christians. — The Mohammedans raise the cry, "Deen, deen, deen Mohammed!" — The Christian Quarter set on fire and the Christians terror-struck. — General Plunder and Spoliation of the Christians. — Huge Deluge of Massacre and Fire. — Abd-el-Kader saves 12,000 Christians. —All the Christians of Syria in danger. — Statistics of the Massacre.—August 3, 1860, Conference of European Powers at Paris.

The bloody orgie was not yet over. On the 9th of July the Mohammedans of Damascus rose upon the Christian population of that city, invaded the Christian quarter, and, with demoniac yells, commenced the work of pillage, burning and massacre. For days previously the Christians had been reviled, menaced and insulted in the bazaars in every possible manner. The great Mohammedan feast of the Beiram was close at hand. On Mount Arafat, the faithful on that day slaughtered sheep, — a propitiatory sacrifice; this year at Damascus they would offer up a worthier propitiation, — they would slaughter Christians. The latter, at last terrified and bewildered, kept to their houses, spending day and night in lamentation and prayer. Seeing no measures of any kind taken by the local authorities to check this fanatical spirit, or to punish such alarming demonstrations, the European consuls appealed in a body over and over again to Achmed Pasha, the governor, to waken to a sense of the danger which hung over the Christian population, and to take the best means for their defence. He first affected ignorance, next pleaded inefficiency of force, and then evinced confusion and alarm at the magnitude of the crisis.

His proceedings had already excited the worst suspicions, and his present language and attitude came in strong confirmation. He had been in constant conference with some of the leading notables of the city famous for their fanaticism. Whenever he went to the mosque, his guard took up their station next the Christian quarter, instead of, as usual, next that of the Mohammedans. He had moved his family into the castle, which he had replenished with cannon, and the garrison of which was doubled,—all steps necessary, as he said, for the protection of the Mohammedans, whom he had certain information were about to be attacked by the Christians! those poor, inoffensive Christians, not one of whom knew how to handle a musket, and who were utterly devoid of arms of any kind whatever. It was evident, from all these strange proceedings,—of the meaning and intent of which there could be no possible doubt,—that the Turks, here as elsewhere, were thirsting for Christian blood.

A Turkish regiment had, with customary circumspection, been ordered into the Christian quarter to *protect* the Christians,—the identical regiment which, one month before, had presided over the massacre at Hasbeya! The souls of the poor Christians sunk within them at the sight: they felt their doom was sealed. Yet, still hoping even against hope, they endeavoured to win the hearts of their protectors. The officers were feasted;—the men were treated. Hundreds of pounds were collected and distributed amongst them, or spent for their gratification. But time wore on; the plot was ripe; the materials were all ready; the actors were impatient to commence their "rôle;" the signal alone was wanting. At last it was given. For some days past wooden crosses had been thrown into the streets, spitted and trampled upon. Numerous complaints had been made by the Christians at this outrage upon their religion, but with no result. At length, on the morning of the 9th of July, three Mohammedan lads were seized and taken up for this offence, and carried to the court of justice. They were sentenced to be put into chains and to go and sweep the Christian quarter. The die was cast.

As the prisoners, accompanied by the police, passed through the bazaars, the excitement amongst the Mohammedans became stronger and stronger every moment. On their approaching the Grand Mosque, the neighbouring shops were all at once closed. Two merchants darted into that building, and had a minute's interview with the chief ulema. On their coming back they raised a wild cry of "Deen, Deen, Deen Mohammed!"* The awful cry was caught up from mouth to mouth; a terrific commotion spread like lightning

* Religion, religion, the religion of Mohammed!

from street to street; all business was abandoned; the shops were closed; and in less than a quarter of an hour an infuriated mob, brandishing guns, swords, axes, and every description of weapon, was in full career towards the Christian quarter. From all directions was seen and heard the rush and running of men armed up to the teeth, and unarmed boys and women; shouts, imprecations on the infidels, the giaours, and cries of " Kill them! butcher them! plunder! burn! leave not one alive! not a house, not anything! Fear not the soldiers; fear nothing; the soldiers will not touch us." *

Scarcely had the infuriated populace began their attack, when a cannon was discharged by the Turkish guard near the Greek church. It was merely loaded with powder, and directed upwards against a mat covering, which stretched over the bazaar. The matting took fire,—a sign that the Christian quarter was to be burned. The work of incendiarism instantly commenced. The wildest confusion now prevailed. The houses were entered and gutted. Large bands ran to

* Further papers relating to disturbances in Syria, p. 37.

and fro carrying off plunder of every description. The people of the suburbs came pouring in. The Turkish soldiers stationed at the gates opened them wide, and invited the intruders to come in boldly. Those who were without arms were refused admittance until they went back and procured them. The supplies of water were cut off. By sunset the whole Christian quarter was in a blaze, the flames waving and mounting, in huge billowy surges, like a sea of fire; while in the midst were seen distracted crowds of women, some carrying infants in their arms, shrieking and rushing along the flat roofs, and springing from house to house. Many lost their footing and fell, breaking their arms or legs, or perishing miserably. The greater part fled through the town, and, rushing wildly into Mohammedan houses, implored the pity of the harem.

Hitherto the ruffians had only thought of plunder. No impediment whatever was offered to their proceedings. The Christians from the commencement appealed to the soldiers for their promised assistance and defence. The officers brutally replied that they had no orders to act.

Presently, to their horror and dismay, they saw the soldiers joining in the attack and carrying off the booty; nay more, putting their bayonets to their breasts and ferociously barring them all means of escape. In whatever direction the affrighted fugitives turned, they were met by steel and fire. Nothing short of a complete and overwhelming destruction seemed to await them. But in the midst of their despair relief came.

An illustrious exile was in that wicked city, spending his days and nights in study, religious meditation and prayer. Patriotic, disinterested, single-hearted, his whole life had been one continued act of devotion, a long and conscientious struggle in the path of duty. Like all great moral sacrifices, his had been sanctified by adversity and misfortune. His brightest laurels were his reverses. Vanquished, he yet wore the victor's wreath, as a martyr his crown. Abd-el-Kader had accepted his destiny with cheerfulness and resignation, and joyfully contemplated his career as finished. But providence had reserved for his brows another and a nobler wreath — a work of mercy — and, Heaven-directed, he arose this day to do the deed that was to shed fresh lustre on his glorious name.*

No sooner had Abd-el-Kader gained intelligence of the frightful disaster, than he sent out his faithful Algerines into the Christian quarter, with orders to rescue all the wretched sufferers they could meet. Hundreds were safely escorted to his house before dark. Many rushed to the British consulate. As night advanced fresh hordes of marauders, Kurds, Arabs, Druzes entered the quarter, and swelled the furious mob of fanatics, who now, glutted with spoil, began to cry out for blood. The dreadful work then began. All through that awful night and the whole of the following day, the pitiless massacre went on.

To attempt to detail all the atrocities that were committed would be repugnant and useless. The violation of women, the ravishing of young girls,— some in the very streets amidst coarse laughs and savage jeers,— some snatched up and carried off. Hundreds of them thus disappeared, hurried away to distant parts in the surrounding country, where

* " And heaven-directed, came this day to do
    The happy deed that gilds my humble name."—HOME.

they were instantly marrried to Mohammedans. Men of all ages from the boy to the old man, were forced to apostatise, were circumcised on the spot, in derision, and then put to death. The churches and convents, which, in the first paroxysm of terror, had been filled to suffocation, presented piles of corpses, mixed up promiscuously with the wounded and only half dead; whose last agonies were amidst flaming beams and calcined blocks of stone falling in upon them with earthquake shock. The thoroughfares were choked with the slain.

To say that the Turks took no means whatever to stay this huge deluge of massacre and fire would be superfluous. They connived at it, they instigated it, they ordered it, they shared in it. Abd-el-Kader alone stood between the living and the dead. Fast as his Algerines brought in those whom they had rescued, he reassured them, consoled them, fed them. He had himself gone out and brought in numbers personally. Forming them into detached parties, he forwarded them, under successive guards, to the castle. There, as the terrific day closed in, nearly 12,000 of all ages and sexes were collected and huddled together, a fortunate but exhausted residue, fruits of his untiring exertions. There they remained for weeks, lying on the bare ground without covering, hardly with clothing, exposed to the sun's scorching rays; their rations, — scantily served out, — cucumbers and coarse bread. Lest they might obtain an unreserved repose, the Turkish soldiers kept alarming them with rumours of an approaching irruption, when they would all be given over to the sword.

Abd-el-Kader himself was now menaced. His house was filled with hundreds of fugitives, European consuls, and native Christians. The Mohammedans, furious at being thus baulked of their prey, advanced towards it, declaring they would have them. Informed of the movement, the hero coolly ordered his horse to be saddled, put on his cuirass and helmet, and mounting, drew his sword. His faithful followers formed around him, brave remnant of his old guard, comrades in many a well-fought field, illustrious victors of the Moulaia.* The fanatics came in sight. Singly he

* On the 18th of December, 1847, Abd-el-Kader, at the

charged into the midst and drew up. "Wretches," he exclaimed, "is this the way you honour the Prophet? May his curses be upon you! Shame upon you, shame! You will yet live to repent. You think you may do as you please with the Christians; but the day of retribution will come. The Franks will yet turn your mosques into churches. Not a Christian will I give up. They are my brothers. Stand back, or I give my men the order to fire." The crowd dispersed. Not a man of that Moslem throng dared raise his voice or lift his arm against the renowned champion of Islam.

The consternation of the Christians throughout Syria, on hearing of these terrific events, was indescribable. In every town, in every village, in every hamlet, the inevitable doom was hourly expected, and all tremblingly awaited their fate. The Mohammedans were fierce and exulting. All believed, more or less, that the Sultan had issued a decree for the extermination of the infidel. All were prepared to do God service in so glorious a

---

head of 2500 of his bravest soldiers, horse and foot, attacked the army of the Emperor of Morocco, 60,000 strong, near the river Moulaia, and entirely defeated it.

cause. In Aleppo the Christians had purchased a temporary immunity from massacre, by paying large sums of money to the leaders of the rabble. But the latter still held their nightly meetings, and, in one instance, had fired on the police. At any moment they might rise.

At Jerusalem the Mohammedans, fortunately divided amongst themselves by party feuds, had as yet been unable to take common measures for an onset; but the spirit was rife.

Throughout Palestine whole villages of Christians, men, women and children, had embraced Mohammedanism, as the only alternative to a certain death. At Acre the Turkish officer in command had issued large supplies of ammunition to the Musselmans, and fixed the day for a massacre of the Christians; but, on the morning of that very day, two Dutch frigates approached the town, and were thus the providential means of preventing the outrage. In every part of Syria the Ottomans stood

> "Like greyhounds in the slips
> Straining upon the start—"

watching the bloody sacrifice, as yet withheld. There seemed to be a general waiting for the fate of Beyrout. Had that town gone, there cannot be a doubt that a wild cry of slay! slay! would have resounded throughout the length and breadth of the land, and the whole Christian race would have been immolated.

But by the end of June line-of-battle ships, frigates and corvettes, from all nations, came successively dropping in, and war steamers cruised about to all points of the coast. The English and French squadrons under Admirals Martin and Jehennes took up their stations off the port of Beyrout in July. Finally, the French military expedition under General Beaufort D'Hautpol, landed on the 16th of August. With the British flag floating on the waters, and the French standards waving on the soil of Syria, the Christians again breathed. Confidence was restored. Those who had fled to foreign shores returned. The future might at last be in a measure guaranteed— but the past!

  11,000 Christians massacred.
  100,000 sufferers by the civil war.
  20,000 desolate widows and orphans.
   3,000 Christian habitations burnt to the ground.
   4,000 Christians perished of destitution.
  2,000,000*l.* property destroyed.

All these accumulated horrors induced by the Turks.

On the 3rd of August, 1860, a conference was held at Paris by the representatives of Great Britain, Austria, France, Prussia, Russia and Turkey. Two protocols were drawn up and signed. The first containing six articles relating to the conditions of the proposed European intervention in Syria. The second, declaring in the most formal manner, "that the contracting powers do not intend to seek for, and will not seek for, in the execution of their engagements, any territorial advantages, any exclusive influence, or any concession with regard to the commerce of their subjects, such as could not be granted to the subjects of all other nations.

"Nevertheless, they cannot refrain, in recalling here the acts issued by the Sultan, the great importance of which was established by Article XI. of the Treaty of March 30, 1856, from expressing the value which their respective courts attach to the fulfilment of the solemn promises of the Porte, that serious administrative measures should be taken to ameliorate the condition of the Christian population of every sect in the Ottoman empire."

And then in the presence, and with the consent of the five aforesaid Christian representatives, — assembled together for the express purpose of taking measures to stop the effusion of Christian blood in Syria, caused by the wicked and wilful collusion of the Sultan's authorities, — the following insult to the common sense, the feelings and judgment of Christian Europe, was deliberately penned.

"The plenipotentiary of the Sublime Porte takes note of this declaration of the representatives of the high contracting powers, and undertakes to transmit it to his court—pointing out—*that the Sublime Porte has employed, and continues to employ, her efforts in the sense of the wish expressed above.*"

On this, let every Briton, who has a head to think and a heart to feel, after perusing the preceding pages, make his own comment.

CHAP. VIII.

Frustration of the Turkish Plan of the *entire* Slaughter of the Christian Male Population. — July 1860, Kurchid Pasha compels the Christian Emirs to sign the Articles of Peace. — July 17th, Fuad Pasha, the Ottoman Extraordinary Commissioner, arrives at Beyrout. — August 16th, the French Division of 7000 arrives. — October 5th, the International European Commission.—July 25th, Vigorous Protest by Admiral Martin. — Inadequate Retribution. — Sept. 12th, Fuad Pasha summons the Druze Sheiks. — Fuad Pasha asks the Christian Deputies for a List of the Druze Offenders. — The List of 4600 Druzes and 360 Mohammedans is made out, but ignored by Fuad Pasha. — A revised List again ignored. — Dec. 8th, mock Trial at Muchtara of Druze Prisoners. — Fuad Pasha asks for a reduced List of 300 Druzes. — Dismissal of the Christian Deputies. — Release of 500 Druze Prisoners. — 120 Druze Culprits are sent to Tripoli, Africa. — Fuad Pasha's Partiality for the Druzes. — The Object of the French Expedition frustrated by Fuad Pasha. — Turkish Treachery and Druze Ferocity unpunished. — June 5th, 1861, Departure of the French Troops.

NEJIB PASHA, who was installed governor of the pashalick of Damascus on the restoration of Syria to the Sultan in 1840, declared to a confidential agent of the British consul in that city, not knowing, however, the character of the person he was addressing, "the Turkish government can only maintain its supremacy in Syria by cutting down the Christian sects." It has been seen that what Nejib Pasha enounced as a theory, Kurchid Pasha, after an interval of twenty years, succeeded in carrying into practice. Not, however, to the extent which had been planned and anticipated: for there can be no doubt whatever that it was the intention of the Turkish authorities in Syria to have carried the work of extermination to far greater limits than those it actually reached. The Druzes are even reviled by some of these functionaries for having spared the few Christians they did.

And, certainly, to judge from the turn affairs have finally taken, from the way in which both Druzes and Mohammedans engaged in the massacres have escaped all punishment worth the name, when compared with their atrocities; and from the manner in which the Porte has benefited, and contrived not only to hold its own, but to accomplish fully and entirely, by means of the ruthless action of its subordinate agents, all the political objects it had in view as regards the Lebanon, it may be considered morally certain, that had Christianity been destroyed root and branch, and utterly extirpated throughout Syria; had every town, and village, and hamlet, throughout the length and breadth of its territory, from Antioch to Gaza, from the Mediterranean to the Euphrates been deluged with Christian blood, the Turks (such are the jealousies, the dissensions, and the materialistic policy of the cabinets of Europe) would have stood absolved from the great abomination, while the principle of the integrity and independence of the "Turkish empire" would have borne them scathless and triumphant along the path of carnage.

As the assassin, after having despatched his victim, muffles up his body, digs a hole, and commits it to the earth, thus propitiating oblivion; so Kurchid Pasha, while the warm blood of his Christian victims was yet steaming up to heaven, summoned to his presence the principal Christian emirs and sheiks, and compelled them to agree to, and sign the articles of a peace based on "complete oblivion of the past." "Consequently," so runs this notable document, "it has been agreed and decided, after invoking the *Divine assistance*, to conclude peace on the condition aforementioned, and that all that has passed from the beginning of the war to the present date (July, 1860) is not liable to any claim or pretension on either side, neither at present nor in future." Thus was the Christian sect to be cut down, the men massacred, the widows and orphans turned adrift to penury and starvation, their habitations ravaged, spoliated, and burnt — and no more to be said about it!

Such was the Turkish programme. And in all probability, had not ulterior circumstances arisen to disturb the harmony of such a procedure, the Turks would have succeeded in carrying it out nearly, if not completely, to the letter. For the British government, at this period, either in complete ignorance, or affecting complete ignorance, of the machinations of the Turkish authorities in Syria, and of their having purposely induced all these disorders, for their own selfish ends, expressed its desire that they should be allowed to manage their own affairs and settle matters as best they could.

News of these heart-rending events had already reached and excited a deep sensation in Europe, when the intelligence of the monstrous tragedy of Damascus swelled the voice of pity into one loud and prolonged cry of horror and execration. Many thought, in their crude simplicity, that the knell of the Ottoman empire had at last sounded. Some Turkish dignitaries, even at Constantinople (amongst those, of course, who had not been initiated into the secrets of the hellish conspiracy), exclaimed, on learning the extent of the disaster, "We are lost." Alas! these sanguine speculators, these gloomy alarmists, had yet to learn the accommodating flexibility of diplomatic Christianity.

The callous stoicism of the British cabinet was at length affected, and a tardy, though hesitating consent was given to the proposal of the Emperor of the French to send an expeditionary force to Syria, for the purpose of aiding in restoring tranquillity, of giving security to the Christians, and of supervising the work of retribution. It now remains to be seen especially, what has been the mode and extent of this retribution, so loudly and so justly called for by the voice of Europe, as well as of the means adopted to indemnify the Christians in some degree for their deplorable losses.*

The following executive was appointed and sent to Syria for the purpose of giving effect to these laudable purposes.

Fuad Pasha, Extraordinary Commissioner from the Sublime Porte, who arrived at Beyrout July 17th, 1860.

A French division consisting of 6000 men, under General Beaufort d'Hautpol, which landed at Beyrout on or about August 16th, 1860.

An international European Commission, consisting of representatives from the five powers, which held its first sitting at Beyrout, October 5th, 1860.

For the sake of perspicuity it will be better to follow the working and operation of these authorities, successively.

For many days after Fuad Pasha had landed, Kurchid Pasha, the massacrer, went about as

* See Syrian Correspondence, 1860–61, pp. 11, 31.

usual, and had even been sent by the former on a mission to Latakia: on his return from whence he was on the point of resuming his functions at Beyrout. A vigorous protest from Admiral Martin at once prevented such a shameless proceeding. There is something so dignified, so high minded, so energetic and uncompromising, so redolent of the lofty spirit of our Blakes and our Nelsons in this admirable "Memorandum," as it was called, that I cannot refrain from transcribing it entirely, as a model of what a despatch to a Turkish authority should be, whether on great or small occasions.

"A most grievous wrong has been inflicted upon the civilised world by the barbarities which have been committed upon the Christian population in Syria.

"The Turkish local authorities have been direct parties to the barbarities, by permitting the soldiers and Moslem population to aid the Druzes, and after the defeat of the Christians to join in murdering the males, and in committing the foulest crimes upon the women and female children.

"The Christian world cannot, and ought not, to leave these enormities unredressed; and it must be evident that it will not rest satisfied with any measure short of that which shall make a recurrence of the enormities impossible.

"The Turkish government will have no claims to consideration if it should not do voluntary and ample justice. The matter will probably be taken out of their hands if they exhibit any indication of shortcoming,

"If they would avoid foreign interference, the limit or consequence of which it may not be difficult to imagine, they must be prompt in declaring that they have, with every other civilised government, an abhorrence of the infamous deeds that have been perpetrated in Syria.

"Their declarations to this effect must be accompanied by acts of full justice to sufferers, and conspicuous retribution to infamous functionaries.

"The mere punishment of humble officials would be deemed an offensive trifling that would have no beneficial influence to restrain the future.

"The highest who have abused their power by participation or connivance in the grievous misery that has been heaped upon the Christian population of Syria, should themselves suffer.

"I have been told that his excellency Kurchid Pasha is to continue in authority in this pashalick. I must express a hope that there is no intention of allowing him to hold the power he has so abused. But looking to the horrible cruelties to which, it is believed, he has been a willing party, and to the responsibilities in which I share with regard to the safety of the Christian population here, I must protest against his being allowed to retain a command upon which the safety of multitudes depends, for whom he has manifested such indifference and contempt.

(Signed) "W. F. MARTIN."

"'Marlborough' at Beyrout, July 25th, 1860."

A few hours after Fuad Pasha received this document, Kurchid Pasha was arrested and thrown into prison. His Kehié, and two other of his subordinates were similarly treated. Nor is it difficult to conceive the influence which this powerful admonition must have had over the subsequent judicial proceedings at Damascus, which city Fuad Pasha entered on the 29th of July, 1860.

It is needless to detail all the measures taken by Fuad Pasha to effect his object of punishing the guilty, but a statement of their results will be significant and instructive.

Achmed Pasha, the governor and military commander of Damascus, convicted on the evidence of a certain Saleh Zechy Bey, a Mohammedan, — who boldly came forward and accused him of gross dereliction of duty, and of having, by his cowardice and impotence, caused the massacre, — was shot. Three Turkish officers who were present at the massacre at Hasbeya, and a hundred and seventeen individuals,—chiefly Bashi-bazouks, police and wandering characters, — met with the same fate. About four hundred of the lower orders were condemned to imprisonment and exile. Of the citizens fifty-six were hanged. Of the notables eleven were exiled to Cyprus and Rhodes, and their property sequestered for the time being. It has since been restored to their families. These notables are living in their places of exile with all the comforts and luxuries of life ; one of them has celebrated his marriage. A sum of about 200,000*l.* was proposed to be levied on the city, a sum which three or four of its principal Mohammedan merchants could furnish alone with ease.

Such is all the amount of retribution which outraged Christian Europe has been able to obtain for the wanton plundering and burning to the ground of the whole Christian quarter of Damascus, entailing a loss to that unfortunate community of at least 2,000,000*l.* sterling,— for the inhuman, savage and cold-blooded massacre of 6000 inoffensive Christians, who possessed no arms whatever,—for the ravishing of their wives and daughters,— and for the expulsion from their desolated hearths of 20,000 beggared and defenceless victims of Mohammedan rage and fanaticism, "whose only crime was," to use the words of the British consul, "that they were the followers of Christ!"

On his return to Beyrout, September 12, Fuad Pasha summoned some of the principal Druze sheiks and notables to appear before him, under penalty of forfeiture of their titles and privileges and sequestration of their properties. Fourteen obeyed the summons; thirty-three refused. The penalty was inflicted on them all indiscriminately, on the former without trial. Kurchid Pasha, Taher Pasha, three other Turkish officials, and seven of the Druze sheiks were accused and examined before an especial tribunal convoked for that purpose. The Turks were sentenced to perpetual imprisonment, the Druzes to death. A like sentence had been previously passed on Abdesclam Bey, the Turkish colonel, who presided at the massacre of Deir-el-Kamar. Four of the Druzes were clearly convicted of having murdered Christians with their own hands. The punishment of death passed on the Druze sheiks has since been commuted to perpetual imprisonment.

None of these sentences have been carried into execution, whether of death or of penal imprisonment.

Fuad Pasha now turned his attention to the punishment of the Druze commonalty. With this view he assembled the Christian bishops, and invoked their assistance to assist him in carrying out a measure so imperatively necessary. He told them that the atrocities committed by the Druzes on the Christians of the Lebanon were known to all the world; that the blood thus shed demanded a bloody retribution, and that they might depend upon his making it with unsparing severity. The bishops replied that they could not, consistently with their sacred calling, interfere in such a case, in which they might, unwittingly, be accessory to the shedding of innocent blood; but that they would name Christian deputies who might give his Excellency the assistance he required. Sixteen deputies were accordingly named. Fuad Pasha, after making them an impressive allocation, — of which the chief feature was most solemn and reiterated assurances of his determination signally to avenge the cause of the slaughtered Christians, — concluded by calling on them to furnish him with a list of those amongst the Druzes who were known to have been the "most barbarous." He pledged himself that whatever passed between him and them should be considered strictly secret and confidential, and made them take a solemn oath on the Bible, in presence of their bishops, that they would discharge the duty they were about to perform faithfully and conscientiously.

After an interval of more than a month,— during which the deputies made the most searching inquiries in every direction, and from all the Christians, whether men or women, who were able to give them the information they required, — they presented Fuad Pasha with a list containing the names of 4600 Druzes and 360 Mohammedans and Metualis, all of whom, they declared, had taken part in the massacre. The place and the nature of his crime was placed opposite the name of each individual.

An insinuation was immediately mooted and spread abroad that the Christian deputies had asked for the heads of 4600 Druzes! — one actively countenanced by, if not indeed emanating from, the Turkish authorities, who were of course only too glad to see the character of the Syrian Christians placed in such a light as would bring upon them the odium, instead of enlisting in their behalf the commiseration of Europe. A more crafty, a more malicious, and, shame be it said, a more successful stroke of policy than this perhaps was never achieved. For absolutely, from this very period, and as a consequence of this accusation, in which the Christian bishops and deputies were alike confounded, the current of public opinion, in some parts of Europe, and especially in England, was completely turned; and English statesmen and legislators, and English journalists and philanthropists vied with each other in unmeasured abuse of the unfortunate Christians, while they sympathised with, and even pressed forward to come to the relief of the Druze assassins.

The bishops protested in the strongest manner against the accusation thus brought against them. The deputies declared they had never been told to make out a death list, but merely a list containing the names of the "most barbarous" of the Druzes. This they had conscientiously done; believing that, having done so, no further action on their part would be necessary, and that the Turkish executive would dispose of that list in the manner best calculated to secure the ends of justice. This list was divided into three categories:—

1. The instigators, whether they took part personally or not in the massacre.
2. Chiefs of bands who headed the assassins, the spoliators and burners.
3. Individuals denounced by public opinion as having committed the principal murders, or of having acted under circumstances aggravating their culpability.

Fuad Pasha now called upon the deputies to revise their lists, which they did. In the revised list the first category contained the names of the most deeply criminal of the Druzes, to the amount of 1200. It was now the general belief and expectation of the Christians at large that these 1200 so denominated would be *executed* in batches on the very scenes of the massacres; and that at least a considerable number of the remaining 3400 Druzes would be sent to the galleys, exiled, and drafted into the Turkish army. Such was their idea of the retribution which ought to overtake the monsters who had committed such outrageous atrocities.

Shortly after the revised list had been given in, a simultaneous seizure took place in numerous villages of about 1500 Druzes. The Christians naturally thought that at last the long-promised punishment of the murderers was about to be effected. What was their surprise and astonishment when, three days later, many of the most savage of the Druze prisoners,—men whose names were known to be on the list as amongst the "most barbarous," were released without the slightest examination, leaving only about 800 in the hands of the authorities. This unaccountable circumstance at once shook their confidence in the sincerity of the government, a feeling which ulterior circumstances only increased.

On the 8th of December, Fuad Pasha proceeded to Mu*ch*tara, as being a central point in the Druze districts, and established an especial tribunal for the trial of the Druze prisoners. He ordered the Christian deputies to follow him. Disgusted with the symptoms of foul play which had already been so clearly evinced, foreseeing the utter inadequacy of the punishment about to be inflicted on the Druze malefactors, as compared with what Fuad Pasha had led them to expect, and indeed, as compared with the exigencies of the commonest justice, the deputies unanimously refused to go. However, eight of them were at last induced to obey the summons.

On being admitted to a private interview, Fuad Pasha requested them to give him such information regarding the Druze prisoners as might assist him in selecting and punishing them, according to their degrees of guilt. They replied, that all the information they had it in their power to give, they had already given in the list they had presented; that they never considered themselves as standing in the position of advocates for the great body of the Christians; that the latter, indeed, and particularly the bereaved widows, had strenuously, and even angrily, refused to put the advocacy of their rights and claims into any deputed hands; and that, consequently, they could in no way enter into questions affecting justice, or give individual evidence, in cases where the lawful complainants were not present.

Fuad Pasha replied, that he in no way whatever meant to impugn, or to doubt for a moment the correctness of their list; that he did not even wish to consider them as advocates for the Christians;

that he looked upon them merely as men of known respectability and influence in their community, and he appealed to them as such, to give what information they could regarding the culpability of the Druzes now in prison. The deputies still adhered to their former statement; adding, however, that they must with all due deference observe, that the bond of secrecy under which his Excellency had formally engaged them to draw up their list, had been broken, inasmuch as that list had been published all over the mountain; and further, that many of the most bloodthirsty Druzes, whose names were down on the list had been seized, and then released. Both these things had given them great disappointment.

Fuad Pasha answered, that if it was true, as they stated, that such characters had been seized and then let loose, the responsibility rested with the officers engaged in effecting their capture, and he should order strict inquiries to be made upon the matter.* He then referred them to the especial tribunal, where, upon presenting them-

* Of course no such inquiry was ever made.

selves, they were called upon, the same as by Fuad Pasha, to give evidence against the Druze prisoners, and in a similar manner declared their utter incompetency to do any such thing. Fuad Pasha again called the deputies before him, told them he thought they were unnecessarily fastidious, that he looked upon them as a kind of jury, an institution in use in civilised countries, and that by associating them in the work of accomplishing the ends of justice, neither they nor he would incur the charge of acting with haste or partiality. He then asked them to draw out, secretly and confidentially, a list of 300 Druzes, most notorious for their ferocity and barbarity, and whose public execution would strike terror.

The deputies replied, that there were so many Christians whose losses had been so severe, and whose claims for reparation were so great (numbers of them having had from five to fifteen near relations massacred), that it would be impossible for them to make out such a list, with anything like an approximation to truth, unless they were allowed to return to Beyrout again and make further inquiries. Fuad Pasha told them they might send for the Christians from whom they wished to make inquiries. "They are so numerous," replied the deputies, "that their being brought hither would be attended with great difficulty and inconvenience." "Then," said Fuad Pasha, "I perceive all your answers are mere evasions, the fact being that you do not wish to comply with my request. As for allowing you to go and collect particular evidence as regards the most notorious of the Druze offenders, that I cannot agree to; it would occupy too much time, and I came up here and established a tribunal, in order to do summary justice. If any of you have any particular accusations to substantiate, I shall be ready to hear them. If not, and you still persist in your refusal, you are at liberty to go; but I warn you that after your departure hence not a single complaint will be listened to against a Druze, by either Christian man, woman, or child."*

And the deputies went away. The following

---

* Two days ago, a Druze was recognised by some of the Hasbeya widows in Sidon, as one who had murdered their day 500 of the Druze prisoners were released, besides some thirty Metualis, notorious assassins, each having a paper given him that he was absolved from all further accusation. A short time afterwards about 240 of the remaining Druze prisoners were exiled to Tripoli on the Barbary coast, for longer or shorter periods, with express instructions that they were to be kindly treated. Thus the great Druze retribution grew "gradually small and beautifully less" and disappearing,

> "Like the baseless fabric of a vision,
> Left not a rack behind."

It is difficult to conceive how the Christian deputies could have acted otherwise than they did. Had they entered upon the functions required of them by the Turkish executive at Muchtara, they would have been placed in an utterly false position, and assumed a responsibility which they could not with any decency have taken upon themselves; as they would thereby have compromised, if not indeed completely sacrificed, the

husbands in the serail before their eyes, and nearly tore him to pieces. He escaped, and was taken before the pasha in that town, who immediately released him! July 1, 1861.

dearest interests and the most solemn rights of the whole Christian community—their most unquestionable and indefeasible rights, be it said, to an extensive and a bloody retribution on the heads of the remorseless shedders of Christian blood. There were scores of Druze assassins, whose names were down on their list, going about, who could easily have been seized, and were not seized. There were scores more who had been seized and were released.

As to the reduced number of 300 Druze criminals to which the process of justice was about to be limited, in the first place, such a number in no way came up to their view of the extent of punishment which the Druze atrocities called for, and which Fuad Pasha had led them to expect; and in the next place, they had formed a pretty good estimate of the kind of justice they were likely to obtain from the especial tribunal at Much'tara (even had the list of 300 been made out and subjected before it to a rigorous investigation), from the proceedings of a trial which had already taken place before that tribunal, in which a Christian woman produced two witnesses to convict a Druze of having murdered her husband, and was subjected to the following frivolous and vexatious questions, turning the forms of justice into a burlesque. "With what instrument did the prisoner kill your husband—with a gun or a sword? Was it a double-barrelled or a single-barrelled gun? Whereabouts did the ball hit him? in the chest or in the side? Did the ball lodge in or pass through his body? Did he fall on his back or on his face?"

If such were the questions put in one case, and regular and satisfactory answers required, what Druze could have been convicted? The woman in question at last turned round to the cadi in indignation and disgust, and said, "You have forgot to ask me one important question, whether my husband went to heaven or to hell!" In fact, the Christian deputies saw clearly they were being made fools of, and that there was no real intention to do the wretched and miserable Christians any kind of justice whatever worth the name. They resolved therefore to wash their hands clean of all participation in such nefarious proceedings, and to leave the common cause of outraged and insulted Christianity in the hands of Him, who "hears the cry of the widow and the oppressed," and who has declared "Vengeance is mine, I will repay!"

The French soldiers landed in Syria on the 16th of August, 1860, singing war songs against the Druzes, and anticipating that they would be forthwith called upon to take an active part in protecting and avenging the unfortunate Christians. After a delay of about a month, spent in the pine wood near Beyrout, they were allowed to make a movement. The chief object in view was the capture of the Druzes, preparatory, as it was loudly proclaimed, to condign punishment. The Turkish troops were reported to have completed a military cordon between the eastern slopes of the Lebanon and the Houran, thus cutting off their retreat in the latter direction. An advance of troops from the western side of the Lebanon, or the sea-side, was all that was requisite to confine the Druzes within a circle from which it was declared they could not possibly escape. On the 24th of September Fuad Pasha ascended into the Druze mountains from Sidon. General Beaufort d'Hautpol, at the head of his troops, divided into two columns of 2,000 men each, made a simultaneous and parallel advance from Beyrout.

Several hundred Christians followed in the track of the French expedition, and committed some excesses. Wound up to a pitch of exasperation which knew no control at the complete impunity which had hitherto attended the cold-blooded barbarities of the Druzes, they slew, it is said, upwards of one hundred of them, including a few women. These deeds were perpetrated out of the French line of march, and consequently escaped notice at the moment. General Beaufort had no executive jurisdiction in the Lebanon; nevertheless, whenever a Christian, convicted even of robbery, was brought before him he was severely handled. Many, on the complaints of the Druzes, suffered corporal punishment for the most petty thefts. The character of the French army for exemplary discipline was consequently in no wise affected by these transactions of the Christians.

After a few days' march through the mountains, the French and Turkish generals descended into the Bekaa, and met at the village of Jib-Jeneen, at the foot of the Anti-Lebanon. It there transpired that owing to some unaccountable, but most convenient, opening made in the military cordon of the Turkish army above alluded to, the Druze sheiks with more than 2000 followers, had succeeded in getting clean away into the Houran. Fuad Pasha endeavoured to console General Beaufort for this disappointment,—this unlooked for "contretemps,"—remarking with winning courtesy and refined sarcasm, that adequate measures had already been taken to capture the offenders, and concluded by inviting him to reascend the Lebanon. General Beaufort, bewildered, perplexed, and sorely chagrined at such a fruitless and ridiculous termination to his co-operative movement, expressed his opinion in no measured terms. But, as he was under Fuad Pasha's orders, nothing was left to him but to accept his colleague's invitation, bid him adieu, and retrace his steps.

"Farewell! Othello's occupation's gone!"

From that day the French were quartered in different villages in the mountain, not exactly turning their swords into pruning-hooks, but acting as masons or as carpenters, in assisting the Christians to rebuild their cottages. The greater part of them spent their time in eating their rations and smoking their pipes; while all were obliged to remain passive and impotent spectators of the unavenged wrongs of the victims of Turkish treachery and Druze ferocity. General Beaufort spent the seven following months at Beyrout, occasionally varying the monotony of his life by promenades in the mountain, occasionally disquieted by insults offered to, and even blows inflicted on his gallant soldiers by Mohammedans, without redress.

At last, "the long deferred but inevitable day arrived." The sun of the 5th of June, 1861, rose resplendent on the French tricolour, but only to shed glorious rays on its humiliation. The brave

Zouaves embarked under cover of night stealthily. A general feeling of commiseration was excited in all breasts at this pitiful exit of the advanced guard of a great nation.

On the 8th, two battalions marched down to the shore in open day with bands playing, but evidently struggling with feelings which French soldiers are fortunately rarely if ever called upon to experience. The weather was hot and sultry. The officers and men in vain strove to hold up their heads and appear animated—their very standards looked drooping, downcast and abashed.

Thus ended the French occupation. That the presence of the French expeditionary force in Syria exercised a most beneficial moral influence cannot be denied. It induced a general feeling of security amongst the Christian population, while it overawed the spirit of Mohammedan fanaticism. On the appearance of the French troops in the mixed districts of the Lebanon, the Druzes were perfectly panic-struck, and fled in all directions: the sheiks hiding themselves in the woods or in caverns, and the women imploring shelter at the hand of the Christians. This state of things continued for more than two months. When, however, the Druzes discovered that the French were not coming to exterminate them, but, on the contrary, treated them with the greatest forbearance, and even gave them assurances of freedom from molestation, they gradually regained confidence and returned to their homes.

That the French were not more practically useful, especially as regarded the seizure and punishment of the Druze malefactors, must be ascribed solely to the jealousy with which their intervention was viewed, from the beginning, by both the British and the Turkish Governments. They had been little more than two months in Syria, when her Majesty's Government declared " that there were insuperable objections to a prolonged occupation ; " and recommended that the pacification of the country should be left entirely to the Turkish authorities; strangely admitting at the same time that " no security would be obtained against a recurrence of the conflicts of Druzes and Christians; for that so long as the two races existed, no permanent security could be obtained."* The

* Correspondence on Affairs of Syria, 1860—61, p. 186.

Turkish Government thus countenanced was not slow in its endeavours to neutralise the intruding element, either by openly rejecting the offers of effective co-operation and assistance made by the French general, or by assuming an attitude of supineness which rendered co-operation impossible.

Deeply indeed is it to be regretted that such unworthy feelings should have been allowed to thwart the action of an expedition which might otherwise have done signal service to the cause of justice and humanity. Had the British Government nobly and magnanimously abjured those suspicions, which the event has proved to have been so groundless, gone straight in for the work of retribution, and, placing before its eyes, as of sacred and paramount importance, the punishment of those who had so cruelly outraged Christianity, given a cordial and unhesitating support to the French intervention, there can be no doubt that the Turkish authority in Syria would have been compelled to have taken very different measures from those it did, and would have been enabled to have accomplished far higher results than what have been achieved. Had such a desirable unanimity of sentiment existed, General Beaufort would never, after having made a fruitless promenade through the Druze mountains in the month of September 1860, been coolly invited " to reascend the Lebanon." An onward movement would have been insisted on, and the Druzes might have been attacked, surrounded, taken and subjected to summary execution in the midst of their strongholds: for the active instigators and perpetrators of the massacres, the "most barbarous" of the Druzes, including many influential chiefs, to the amount of more than 2000 men, had all retreated into the Houran, only four days' march from the Lebanon.

Had Fuad Pasha stationed himself at Damascus, and from thence issued orders for an expedition into the Houran, its success, as far as depended on human calculations, was certain. The period of the year was favourable, the Arab tribes, always more or less in a state of warfare with the Druzes of that district, would have lent their aid against them; and the more eagerly on the present occasion, because they were known to be laden with booty; while a French and Turkish column of 5000 men each, with their full complement of cavalry and artillery, and commanded by such dashing, able and experienced officers as Generals Beaufort and Kmety, marching by combination on the Houran, and, if necessary, even into the heart of the Ledja*, would have left the Druze brigands and assassins merely the alternative of death on the field, or submission. Chastisement would thus have been signally inflicted on the most notorious delinquents, the claims of justice promptly and gloriously satisfied, European honour and superiority vindicated, and, greatest boon of all to England and the Porte, the French occupation, instead of being prolonged might have been shortened.†

---

* A stony, barren district in the Houran, to which the Druzes usually retire as a last resource.

† Since the above chapter was written the Turkish officials and the Druze sheiks condemned to the commuted sentence of imprisonment for life have been removed to Constantinople; but no one imagines for one moment that the punishment, *as for life*, will be carried out.

CHAP. IX.

October 5, 1860, First Meeting at Beyrout of the European Commission. — March 5, 1861, the Twenty-fifth and last Meeting. — The charitable Contributions from Europe. — Lord Dufferin advances from his private Purse 5000*l*. — The Compensation discussed. — The distracted widows of Damascus, Hasbeya, and Rascheya. — Lord Dufferin's sense of Justice and Indignation ; he demands prompt Punishment. — The Slaughter of 5000 human Beings remains unpunished. — Sudden Sympathy for the Druzes. — Guilt of the Turkish Officers proved. — General Reprieve of the Criminals. — Appeal to Christian Europe for Justice.

EARLY in the month of July 1860, the British and French cabinets, on the suggestion of the latter, agreed to make a proposal to the Turkish Government, that a Commission of Delegates from the Porte and from the great powers should be sent to the Lebanon, for the purpose of investigating the circumstances attending the recent acts of violence in that district. This Commission was to have for its object, to determine the responsibility of all persons connected in these proceedings;

to consider what punishment or compensation might be due; and, finally, to submit to the Sultan their opinion upon the measures best calculated to prevent further calamities.*

The Porte had long admitted the principle of European intervention in the affairs of the Lebanon, and though it naturally would have preferred an independent action for its judicial and administrative capacity in the disturbed province, yet, as the precedent had been unquestionably established, it had nothing left but to submit with the best graces it could, consoling itself, no doubt, with the hope, that by the exercise of its usual adroitness, it would succeed in making the Commission subservient to its own purposes. If the operation of the Commission were incommoding, the Porte might thwart or paralyse it; or, with so many elements of discord to preclude unanimity, the Porte might easily make it the scapegoat for its own shortcomings. Under such auspices, the International European Commission for Syria held its first official meeting at Beyrout, October 5th, 1860.

* Syrian Correspondence, 1860—61, p. 6.

Sad satire, it must be admitted, on the notable doctrine of "non-intervention!" Whoever first broached that doctrine, or induced the British Government to adopt it, must be held mainly responsible for the late calamities in Syria.

For, had the British Government intervened during the preceding three years in the affairs of the Lebanon, as it ought to have done, and as it was bound both by principles of right, and by feelings of honour to have done, more than any other European power, inasmuch as in 1840 it solemnly guaranteed to the Lebanon its welfare and happiness; had it condescended to notice, and to profit by the valuable information constantly forwarded to it during that period by its consular authorities, as well as the timely warnings they repeatedly gave; and had it promptly and firmly insisted at the Porte on the removal of those functionaries whose proceedings it was clearly given to understand were inevitably tending to throw the Lebanon into confusion and disorder, nothing of all that has happened could possibly have occurred. But instead of this, madly thinking to bring about a new era of strength and independence to the Ottoman empire, by enforcing the doctrine of "non-intervention," it sunk into a state of utter supineness and indifference as to the well-being of that important district, only to be awoke to a sense of duty by the horrors of war, conflagration and massacre.

The labours of the Commission extended over a space of five months, its last and twenty-fifth meeting taking place March 5th, 1861.* During this period it was occupied, as far as its inadequate powers permitted, in the general work of reorganisation; of endeavouring to restore the scattered Christians to their homes; of rebuilding their ruined tenements; of fixing the amount of their pecuniary indemnities; of supervising all the criminal procedures against the inculpated Turkish authorities and the Druze malefactors; and lastly, of framing such a plan of government for the Lebanon as might bid fair to give its inhabitants that peace, order, and security which they had been vainly invoking for twenty years.

* The members of the Commission were as follows:— Fuad Pasha for Turkey; Lord Dufferin and Claneboye for England; M. Béclard for France; M. Novikow for Russia; M. Weckbecker for Austria; M. Rehfues for Prussia.

It would be useless to attempt to describe the aggravated wretchedness, the intensity of suffering which at one time impended over the miserable widows and orphans who thronged from the scenes of massacre to Beyrout and Sidon. The Druzes laughed at their desolation, taunted them with their calamity, and savagely told them they had been spared that "their hearts might bleed!" The Turks, after having accomplished their fell object, had withdrawn callously from the theatre of carnage. The pall of death seemed to be gradually overshadowing the emaciated forms of these wretched outcasts; and had no friendly hand been extended, they would literally have perished by thousands of sheer starvation. Let this appalling fact be remembered, whenever the mind, horror-struck, unforgetful and unforgiving, thinks of the authors and instigators of this gigantic outrage against Christianity. The charitable contributions which fortunately poured in from Europe on the first news of the great disaster, and especially from France and England, as well as from America, soon spread their vivifying streams over the arid waste of blank despair; and an Anglo-American committee was formed for the management of the funds, which, by its untiring and indefatigable energy, contrived to stem the torrent of destitution.

Lists of the bereaved sufferers were made out according to their villages and districts. Pecuniary assistance was given at the rate of two shillings per head·; large quantities of flour as well as of clothing were distributed; hospitals were established; and every possible measure taken to alleviate the general distress. The Turkish authorities also contributed their modicum of relief; but how utterly inadequate were their means compared with the necessities of the occasion, may be judged from the fact, that in the month of November their funds completely failed, and the daily rations they issued would have been altogether stopped, had not Lord Dufferin in the handsomest manner come forward, and advanced them a loan from his own private purse of 5000*l*., to rescue the unfortunate recipients of Turkish charity from starvation.

The Commission directed its attention, in the first place, to the question of Christian indemnities, which, including the losses incurred at Damascus, in the Lebanon and the surrounding country, were estimated at nearly three millions sterling. In the month of December 1860 it adjourned to Damascus, in order to form some idea of the extent of destruction which had there occurred. On its return to Beyrout it applied itself assiduously to the task of calculating the amount of contribution which it would be feasible to raise from the non-Christian populations most implicated in the work of spoliation and massacre, and of devising the best manner for carrying that object into practice. The losses of the Christians of Damascus alone were estimated in the first place at one million and a quarter, but this estimate was afterwards reduced to 700,000*l.* as a minimum; (the price of lost jewellery, which was enormous, not included), and it was determined that this sum should be exacted from the Mohammedans of that Pashalick. A proposal was made by the Ottoman Commissioner to levy a contribution on the Druzes, but it was over-ruled.

Still, after all the local endeavours that could be

made to realise the requisite amount, it was manifest that an immense deficit would remain to be provided for. The Commissioners would, no doubt, have succeeded in clearing their way to a tangible result, or, at all events, have finally resolved on some measure which would have given the unfortunate Christians some chance of obtaining their due, and of touching an adequate compensation, when, to their surprise, towards the close of their fifteenth sitting, Fuad Pasha informed them that the whole question of the indemnities had been transferred to Constantinople. His Government, he declared, reserved to itself the right of deciding on the manner in which the indemnities should be fixed and paid, as well as the repartition of imposts necessary to their being raised. Thus this important question, on which the future welfare, nay, even the future existence of thousands of Christians depended, was summarily taken out of the hands of those men who by being on the spot were the best able to judge of it in all its bearings; in whose hands, indeed, it ought to have been exclusively left; and whose decision, as regarded every separate indemnity, ought to have been final and without appeal. The Commissioners alone should have possessed this uncontrolled power in apportioning the indemnities, because the Turkish authorities, themselves the authors of all the calamities, and perfectly indifferent as to the ultimate fate of the sufferers, if left to their own inspirations, would naturally endeavour to reduce the amount of compensation to the lowest possible figure. As it was, the adjudication was referred to the Porte, where, as a matter of course, it would be ignorantly and prejudicially discussed, and settled, if settled at all, not on principles of a generous commiseration, but on those of a heartless and unfeeling economy.

It is a matter of surprise that the Commissioners did not at once indignantly refuse to submit to such an insulting nullification of their undoubted prerogative, and declare their determination to refer to their courts for fresh instructions on the subject. In fact, there was but one course for the Commission to have pursued from the beginning, and that was, to have drawn up a report stating the full amount of indemnity which, on the largest and most liberal scale, the Christians required; and then to have pointed out, in the strongest manner, that the only possible way in which that indemnity could ever be obtained, would be by one or two of the great powers advancing the whole sum as a loan to the Turkish Government, compelling it, at the same time, to hypothecate the Syrian revenues for the repayment of the money advanced.

In place of taking this firm and decided step, the French Commmissioner, speaking the sense of his colleagues, expressed the astonishment and profound regret which such a decision had inspired, since it would necessarily induce delays in the execution of a measure which all the members of the Commission unanimously considered "to be of the most vital importance."* The result was exactly what any child could have foretold. After a lapse of two months, the Ottoman Commissioner informed the Commission that the Porte, looking to the slenderness of its resources, could not afford to pay the Christians of Damascus more than 350,000*l.* and that even that sum could only be paid in six months' instalments over a space of three years.

* Syrian Correspondence, 1860—61, pp. 313, 314.

It is doubtful whether this pittance will ever be scraped together; and even such sums as have been collected are distributed more with a view to bribe certain of the Christians to collusion in the heartless robbery, than in the spirit of equity and justice. The heads of the clergy and a few of the notables more immediately under the influence of the Government have received their indemnification nearly in full, putting their seals, in exchange, to documents attesting that ample justice is being done; while, after waiting for nearly a year, the poor traders and artificers, whose sole living is from hand to mouth; the wretched widows and orphans, who have no earthly means of subsistence whatever, are put off with paper promises of payment, on the principle laid down by the Porte—the payment not amounting to a quarter, and, in some cases, not to a tenth part of their established claims, and the paper not being given to them until they have signed receipts to the effect that they have been paid in full.

When this iniquitous procedure was first promulgated, the miserable sufferers, appalled and panic-stricken, knew not which way to turn for consolation and relief. The distracted widows filled the air with their indignant cries of remonstrance; for they clearly foresaw that the unjust pittance about to be given them in successive instalments, would gradually, as it came in, be consumed to supply their daily wants; and that when all was thus expended they would be left, friendless and houseless, to embrace abject penury or certain death. Hundreds thronged the European consulates imploring their assistance and interference to save them from this crushing blow, but only to be farther tortured by useless expressions of commiseration and inability to help. The Christians of the Lebanon are all in a similar predicament, as regards their indemnities;—helpless victims of a spoliation and injustice which the Porte ruthlessly commits, and which Europe, to all appearance, callously sanctions.

The poor widows of Hasbeya and Rascheya, in the anti-Lebanon, had hoped indeed that the sale of their olive crops would have brought them in a small competence, which would have enabled them to struggle on for a few months; for the Turkish authorities had undertaken to protect the crops from the Druzes, and to have them gathered in at the proper season: but instead of receiving eight hundred untars, the regular produce, they are told that there are no more than thirty-five untars, and even these they have not received. And, to complete all, they have been ordered to return to their homes, without the slightest arrangement being made either for giving them shelter and covering, or for providing for their future subsistence: — return to their homes where their houses are still heaped up together in burnt and blackened masses of crumbling ruins, and where the bones of their murdered and unrevenged husbands, brothers and sons are bleaching in the mid-day sun! Such are the tender mercies of the Turks! And all this unblushing swindling and oppression is perpetrated, and all these shameless proceedings go smoothly on, almost in the presence of a French army, and actually in the presence of the combined fleets of England and France!

As one of the main instructions issued to the Commission was, that it should inquire into the circumstances attending the recent civil war, and determine the responsibility of all persons connected with its proceedings, it appeared to the Commissioners indispensable that they should be kept acquainted with all judicial processes, whether against the Turkish functionaries, or the Druze chiefs and commonalty; and more than that, they insisted that agents on their parts should attend the trials, and that not a sentence should be carried into execution without their sanction and approval. The Ottoman Commissioner considered such pretensions to be inadmissible, and expressed his opinion that the Commission should confine its labours exclusively to the "general investigation," as any interference in the "judicial investigation" might affect the independence of the tribunal appointed to try the accused. The firmness of the British Commissioner at once defeated this attempt of the Turkish authorities to free themselves from a control which would necessarily thwart any plans they might entertain of making the ends of justice subservient to the gaining of a political triumph. The proceedings in the trials of the Druze chiefs indeed, already commenced, clearly exhibited such a tendency.

- Lord Dufferin declared, that if the right of the Commission to a full participation in all the judicial investigations was not immediately conceded, he should present himself formally at the doors of the court-house, in order that the responsibility of refusing him admission might rest entirely with the Turkish authorities.* His colleagues unanimously supported him in this view of the rights which belonged to them. Fuad Pasha, then at Damascus, was forthwith informed of the attitude they had thus assumed, and the next mail from that city brought the information that he had yielded the point. At their fifth meeting, October 23rd, 1860, the following formula was drawn up, as a basis for their future conduct:—

"The Commission assumes a collective action, both as regards the inquiry into the causes and origin of the late events, and as regards the guilt and culpability of the leaders of the insurrection, and of the agents of the Turkish authorities."†

Although the right of intervention, which the Commissioners had thus successfully vindicated

---

* Syrian Correspondence, 1860—61, p. 189.
† Ibid. p. 206.

for themselves, was founded on the best motives, and in some measure prevented the perpetration of wrong; yet it undoubtedly in no slight degree impeded the march of justice, and mainly contributed to that extraordinary, and unparalleled *dénouement*, in which the Syrian trials of every description, as far as regarded the Lebanon, ended.

The enormities enacted by the Druzes were so notorious, their authors so well known, the evidence to convict them so abundant and so attainable, that justice had only to strike with her sword, as well as hold her scales, blindfolded, to have effected a fair and ample retribution. But weeks and months rolled on, and the Ottoman Commissioner still seemed perfectly unconscious of the imperative duty he was called upon to perform. The Commission at length became impatient and almost ashamed of the passive "rôle," assigned to it, and feeling the great responsibility it would incur by even the semblance of connivance at such an unaccountable, not to say suspicious, delay, earnestly urged the adoption of speedy and decisive measures. Fuad Pasha, on his part, contented himself by giving the Commissioners repeated assurances of his intention to proceed with the work of punishment; and throwing out the word "to-morrow," with an energy which to their unripe experience seemed pregnant of instant action, left them to follow at their leisure that excruciating "will o' the wisp" of Turkish diplomacy.

Her Majesty's Commissioner was the first to awaken to a full sense of the folly, not to say ignominy, of this delusive chase, and in an admirable interpellation to Fuad Pasha*, gave him to understand that patience had its limits, and that the demands of Europe could no longer be postponed. With just surprise and indignation his Lordship exclaims: "Within the limits of the Lebanon 5000 human beings have been put to the edge of the sword, 200 villages have been burnt, and not a single individual concerned in these atrocious acts has suffered for his crimes! Yet for weeks the Sultan's troops have been in undisputed occupation of the mountain, and months have elapsed since your Excellency's arrival in the province gave promise that the day of retribu-

* Syrian Correspondence, 1860—61, p. 225.

tion was at hand." Again: "Policy and justice alike require that punishment should be inflicted with the utmost celerity." "On this occasion such a signal example should be given as shall for ever convince these Lebanon tribes that from henceforth, neither the Sultan's Government nor Europe will permit a repetition of similiar atrocities."

Lord Dufferin was even of opinion that Fuad Pasha's "delay in punishing the Druzes was to be accounted for, partly, by a feeling of compunction in dealing too harshly with a people whose excesses, his conscience tells him, have been encouraged by officers of the Porte."* This, perhaps, was striking the right chord. For if the Druzes were instruments, and who can doubt it, no one probably knew better than the Sultan's Minister for Foreign Affairs *whose* instruments they were!

The Commission, a few days afterwards, and at its tenth sitting†, unanimously responded to the sentiments so ably expressed by the British Commissioner. With one accord they voted that the

---

* Syrian Correspondence, 1860—61, p. 273.
† Ibid. p. 242.

punishment of the Druzes ought to be prompt and summary: regular procedures would be misplaced: it was necessary to strike quick and hard: the Druzes ought to be proceeded against summarily, militarily, without attending in any way to the ordinary rules of judicial processes: an immediate example was absolutely necessary. The Ottoman Commissioner, affecting to warm up to the occasion, and to be inspired with the enthusiasm of justice then displayed, begged anxiously to be informed whether the Druze malefactors, after they had been seized, should be assembled together at Beyrout previous to execution, or whether he should establish an ambulatory tribunal in the mountain, which, moving about from place to place, and to the very spots even of the late massacres, should strike off heads as it went along! The British Commissioner demanded in the name of humanity, that the condemned, on being led out to receive the fatal blow, should not be unnecessarily tortured by repeated cuts of the sword.

To all appearances the European Commissioners had gained their point. In a few days more Druze heads would roll off by scores. The

Turks, despite their religious scruples, their misgivings and evasions, would be compelled to avenge the shedding of Christian blood in the Lebanon. Outraged Christianity would be appeased. But their Ottoman colleague was skilful in fence. At the conclusion of the sitting, he mildly suggested to the Commission, that, as the trials of the Druze sheiks at Beyrout were still pending, it would be better to await their result, before dealing with the Druzes in the mountain (as if the two matters were in the slightest degree connected). The plea was admitted, the suggestion adopted. A deadly thrust had been made at him. The parry was skilful. He had gained time, and that, with the Turk, is as good as nine points out of twelve in the game.

And now was exhibited with consummate art, before the eyes of the Commissioners, and those of the native Christians, that specious and illusive machinery which has been treated of in the preceding chapter. The calling in of bishops, the naming of notables, the secret pledges, the solemn oaths, the drawing up of lists, the returning of lists, the revision of lists, the seizure of Druzes, the mighty promises made, the large expectations held out, the decking out of justice in gorgeous raiment and glorious apparel: but, in the end, alas! to be mocked at, spat upon and buffeted.

Suddenly, from certain mysterious sources, sprung up a stream of sympathy for the Druzes. The atrocities which those butchers had committed; the thousands of Christians they had murdered, with every possible aggravation of cold-blooded and relentless barbarity; the women they had hacked to pieces; the infants they had torn asunder at the mother's breast; their having deliberately rushed from their own field of blood to stir up the massacre at Damascus, which, but for their hellish agency, would never have occurred*; their having stood in picked bands at the gate of that city, with bared arms and grasping their deadly yatagans, howling for admission to the castle, there to satiate their thirst for Christian blood, even yet unslaked, by the slaughter of all the poor fugitives assembled within its

---

* Abd-el-Kader drew Fuad Pasha's attention to this notorious fact at their first interview.

precincts: all those appalling facts were well nigh submerged.

For what were the Druzes to blame? it became the fashion to say. All they had done was in self-defence. Had not the Maronites for years past been crouching like tigers ready to spring at their throats? Was it not the Maronites who began the war? Had they not, also, committed barbarities? Had they not coolly killed some dozens of Druzes, when following the French army into the mountain? Would they not, had they gained the day, have committed excesses at least equal to, if not exceeding, those committed by the Drues? Were there not Christian criminals as great, if not greater, than the Druzes? Finally, had they not demanded 4600 Druze heads? the monsters! Had not the Druzes been already severely punished? Had they not for months been wandering about their mountains like wild beasts, the sword suspended over their heads, or hiding themselves in caves of the earth, feeding on black bread made of acorns*, and on the roots of the field.

* This black bread the Druzes made for the occasion, to impose upon the credulous who inquired into their condition.

The Turks were in raptures at this revulsion of feeling. Perhaps, after all, the ambulatory tribunal might be established for Christians as well as Druzes. Certain it is, opinions of this nature at last found an echo in the heart of the Commission itself. The plan of summary procedure against the Druzes was abandoned. The greatest alarm was entertained lest one of these unfortunate victims should be put to death innocently. To guard against so frightful a contingency, it was resolved that no Druze should be capitally tried, except on the charge of having murdered in cold blood an unarmed man, woman, or child, and that the evidence of two eye-witnesses should be considered necessary to secure a capital conviction.

In the mean time the trials of the Turkish officials and Druze sheiks at Beyrout had been brought to a close.

Lord Dufferin, in his interpellation to Fuad Pasha, had made use of the following remarkable expressions:—

"Amongst the three classes of criminals who stand arraigned at the bar of Europe, the guilt of those Turkish officers and magistrates, whose apathy or connivance intensified the horror of what it was their duty to have prevented, must ever remain pre-eminent." The cue was thus obtained, as to the opinion entertained by the British Commissioner, at least, with regard to the conduct of the Turkish officers implicated in the late events. It was evident that any sentence, to meet his approval, must place those officers in the first class of criminals, and visit them with the highest degree of punishment. The Austrian Commissioner was known to be averse to any executions whatever. The other Commissioners were known to be prepared to exact the utmost rigour of the law. By sentencing, therefore, the Druze sheiks to death, and the Turkish officials merely to imprisonment, not only would the apple of discord be flung into the midst of the Commission, but the chances were that all the criminals who had appeared before the tribunal would benefit by the dissension thus created.

The effect produced by this manœuvre was exactly what had been anticipated. From the moment the sentences so framed were promulgated, the Commission became engaged in interminable disputes and altercations on the subject, and could never arrive at any decision whatever. Fuad Pasha now proceeded to Muchtara, leaving the Commissioners to extricate themselves as best they could out of the *fourches caudines* into which they had been dexterously thrust.

The proceedings at Muchtara have been so amply recorded that any further allusion to them is unnecessary. It should be remarked, however, that by what Fuad Pasha called " a summary process," to which the activity and vigilance of Colonel Fraser not a little contributed, twenty-five Druzes had been condemned to death, on the clearest and most unquestionable evidence, for having, each one of them, slain in cold blood more than a dozen Christians. The immediate execution of these blood-thirsty savages was strongly called for. Fuad Pasha, however, on the plea that a repetition of executions would not have the same effect as one grand execution on one and the same day, at various places throughout all the mountain, suggested that the Druze malefactors at Muchtara should not be executed until the fate of the Druze sheiks at Beyrout had been determined. The crafty suggestion was adopted. Another delay, and again time gained.

The Ottoman Commissioner returned to Beyrout to find the Commission in all the throes of an impossible delivery. Each Commissioner would study and pour over the " procès-verbal " of the trials separately; then all the Commissioners would lay their heads together and read them over collectively; then they would call in the members of the tribunal to assist them in their lucubrations: all to no purpose. In common parlance, they could make neither head nor tail of the whole affair.

The Austrian Commissioner thought the Turkish officers accused had done their duty. The Prussian was for putting to death Turks and Druzes alike. The Russian had a pocket tribunal of his own, and rejecting the proceedings of the Turkish tribunal, as absurd and derisory, gathered his own information as to the culpability of all the criminals, and founded on it his own decision. The French only wanted two Druze heads, but made a deadly tilt at the head of that precious exemplar of the Druze aristocracy, Said Bey

Jumblatt, to whose rescue, however, the British Commissioner advanced with a spirit of chivalry worthy of a better cause, not objecting, at the same time, to the execution of some thirty or forty of the smaller Druze fry. The field of disquisition was evidently becoming more and more contracted every day. In place of being discussed on the broad principles of justice and humanity, it was gradually being fought out on the narrow basis of political jealousy and contention.

It was absolutely necessary that all this unseemly bickering should be brought to a close. Accordingly, at the twenty-fourth meeting of the Commission, March 2nd, 1861, the Ottoman Commissioner, after having for six mortal hours patiently withstood a galling cross-fire from his European colleagues, stepped forward and expressed " his deep regret that the revision of the processes to which the Commission had applied themselves had led to no result, and that the divergence of opinion was as great as ever. Under these circumstances he had nothing to do but to refer the whole subject to Constantinople."*

* Syrian Correspondence, 1860—61, p. 506.

Another delay and again time gained! Often previously when asked by anxious inquirers when the executions were to begin, he would naively reply, "when these gentlemen have made up their minds."

And to Constantinople, in effect, the whole mass of the judicial investigations was sent. There the bubble burst. *With the consent of the Christian powers*, the great Druze-Mohammedan retribution ended in a general reprieve for criminals, murderers and assassins of every sect, class and degree, engaged in the massacres — *not a hair of one of whose heads has been, or is to be touched:* even including the barbarous Mohammedans of Sidon, who were tried, and clearly convicted of having, without any provocation whatever, but merely out of a wild and fanatical hatred to their religion, ruthlessly slaughtered the men and violated the women of the poor Christian fugitives who fled from the mountain to that city for shelter!

Christian readers! Is not all this monstrous? is it not incredible? is it not heartless? is it not degrading to our common faith? is it not inhuman?

Christian peoples! Have you yet to learn that the best interests of Christianity, in those regions once hallowed by the presence of the Lord and Saviour of mankind, are sacrificed on the altar of diplomacy — frittered away by diplomatists vainly struggling against the wiles which circumvent them, and paralysed by the very power they crudely affect to regulate and guide?

Christian emperors and kings! How long will you continue to desecrate the sacred cause you so ostentatiously pretend to espouse, and to bring contumely, reproach and disaster on the Christians of the East, by your spurious protection, your baneful jealousies, your selfish intrigues, and your blundering ambitions? How long will you tarnish your crowns, sully your sceptres, and put the name of Christ to open shame, by submitting to be led captives of the Turk?

NOTES.

Note 1. — The pronunciation of *ch* in Mu*ch*tara and Za*ch*lé, is the same as the German, Welsh or Spanish guttural sound. The spelling of the name Beshir (the sh pronounced rather sharper than the English sh) was rendered in the "Mount Lebanon" Bechir; Shehab was spelt Shehaab; Beit-ed-deen was spelt Ebtedeen.

Note 2. — In the sixth chapter, the amount of Christians massacred at "Rascheya" in the serail should be stated as 700 in place of 250.

Note 3. — In the same chapter, speaking of the taking of Za*ch*lé, I stated that the Druzes formed an escort to conduct the Christian women out of the town. In this place, the following *foot-note* was omitted: —

* "While giving the Druzes credit for their general forbearance towards the women, I must at the same time state that at Hasbeya and Deir-el-Kamar many old women, some indeed, bed-ridden, and several young girls, were butchered by them in the most inhuman and ferocious manner. Even to the women they spared they savagely exclaimed, 'We spare your lives that your hearts may burn!'"

POSTSCRIPT.

SINCE the above was written, a mixed Commission, in which her Majesty's Government is most ably represented by Colonel Fraser, has been sitting alternately at Damascus and Beyrout, for the verification of the claims of the Christians for losses sustained in Damascus and the Lebanon. A year and a half has elapsed since it commenced its labours, but nothing like an adequate compensation has yet been awarded. The desire of the Ottoman Government to bring down the indemnities to the lowest possible figure, has hitherto defeated, and will continue to defeat, the best intentions on the part of the European Commissioners to procure justice.

OFFERED FOR SALE BY
BERNARD QUARITCH, 15 PICCADILLY.

MOUNT LEBANON:

A TEN YEARS' RESIDENCE, FROM 1842 TO 1852;

DESCRIBING

THE MANNERS, CUSTOMS, AND RELIGION OF ITS INHABITANTS,

WITH A FULL AND CORRECT ACCOUNT OF THE

DRUZE RELIGION,

And containing HISTORICAL RECORDS of the MOUNTAIN TRIBES, from Personal Intercourse with their Chiefs and other Authentic Sources.

By COLONEL CHURCHILL,
STAFF OFFICER ON THE BRITISH EXPEDITION TO SYRIA.

Third Edition, 3 vols. 8vo. 1853.

With a large folding MAP of the Mountain Range of the LEBANON, as surveyed by the Staff Officers in the British Expedition to Syria, 1840; PORTRAITS of Emir Beshir Shehab, late Prince of the Lebanon; of Sheik Ameenadeen, Druze Ockal; of Sheik Yoosuf il Haazin, Patriarch of the Maronites; and VIEWS of Howarra, seat and property of Colonel Churchill; of Muchtara, seat and property of Sheik Said Jumblatt; and of Ebtedeen, palace of the Emir Beshir Shehab.

Published at 25s.; now, in cloth, 15s.

Rich in classical as well as scriptural associations, and full of Eastern anecdote and romance, nowhere can the eye embrace such scenes of absorbing interest as those which burst upon the view from the heights of Lebanon.

Yonder azure mountains, which blend so softly with the ethereal skies around them, enclose the scenes of His career, whose weapons were the Words of Peace; whose doctrines fell on the hearts of His followers like the gentle dews of Heaven, with ever fresh and invigorating influence, summoning them to patience, humility, and endurance, as the ensigns of their warfare and the basis of their triumphs; and who consigned to them the mission—sacred, and lasting as the world itself—of uniting together the great family of mankind in one common bond of Faith, Charity, and Love.

"The glory of the Lebanon shall come unto thee."—ISAIAH, lx. 13.

CONTENTS.

VOL. I.—An Account of the Aristocratic or great Feudal Families, and their Government; the Natural Produce of the Country, and its Topographical Divisions; the Early History of the Mountain Tribes, and their participation in the Crusades; full Particulars of the Ancient Druze Writers and their Works, &c.

VOL. II. contains an elaborate Exposé of the Druze Religion, its History, Doctrines, and Administration, based upon original Druze Manuscripts,—and a History of the Lebanon, from the earliest times to the death of that noble-minded Arab, Emir Fakaradeen Maan, 1635.

VOL. III. contains the Modern History of the Maronites and Druzes, their endless struggles amongst themselves and against their Ottoman rulers. The full particulars of the atrocities committed by DAHER, the Metuali Sheik of Acre, 1770,—and of DJEZZAR, the Butcher, Pasha of Acre, 1788,—the History and many Vicissitudes of Emir BESHIR SHEHAB, 1788-1830, will be read with much interest.

To these three volumes should be added—

VOL. IV.—The DRUZES and the MARONITES under the TURKISH RULE (1 vol. 8vo. LARGE PAPER), forming a continuation or Supplement to the "Mount Lebanon, 3 vols." With a GENERAL INDEX to the 4 vols., *printed uniformly*. Cloth, 10s. 1862.

*** Price of the 4 volumes, 8vo. *Map and Plates, cloth extra*, 25s.; or half-morocco, gilt tops, 30s.

www.ingramcontent.com/pod-product-compliance
Lightning Source LLC
Chambersburg PA
CBHW032053230426
43672CB00009B/1575

ORIENTAL BOOKS
PUBLISHED BY
BERNARD QUARITCH, 15 PICCADILLY.

Arabic Dictionary.

AN ARABIC-ENGLISH AND ENGLISH-ARABIC DICTIONARY. By JOSEPH CATAFAGO, Esq., of Aleppo, Syria; Secretary to Soliman Pasha, Major-General of the Egyptian Army in Syria, 1839-40; First Interpreter to the General Consulate of his Majesty the King of Prussia, at Beirut, 1842-1851; Secretary of the Imperial Grand Consulate of Russia, at Beirut, 1851-53; Corresponding Member of the Sociétés Asiatiques of Paris and Leipsic; also of the Syro-Egyptian Society of London; Translator of the "Catechism of the Ansari," presented to his Majesty the King of Prussia in 1845, and of other Arabic Manuscripts. 2 vols. small 8vo. Vol. 1, pp. 328; Vol. 2, pp. 752, in double columns, much matter compressed into a small space, all the Arabic words with the pronunciation in Roman letters (pub. at £2), cloth, 30s. 1858

The Same. 8vo. Large Paper (pub. at £3. 3s.), half-morocco. £2. 2s.

*** This Work is the first Arabic and English Dictionary ever published.

"A valuable publication. A work of this kind has been long wanting, and Mr. Layard is convinced that Mr. Quaritch has rendered not only good service to those who wish to study the Arabic language, but to such Easterns as wish to obtain a knowledge of English."—*A. H. Layard.*

Arabic Grammar.

FARIS'S PRACTICAL GRAMMAR of the ARABIC LANGUAGE; with Interlineal Reading-Lessons, Dialogues, and Vocabulary, by FARIS-EL-SHIDIAC, a Native of Mount Lebanon, Syria; formerly Professor of Arabic at the University of Malta; Translator of the whole Bible into Arabic; Author of "An English Grammar for Arabs," and of the Arabic work called "The Fariyac." 1 vol. 12mo. cloth, 5s. 1856

Turkish Dictionary.

REDHOUSE'S ENGLISH-TURKISH LEXICON. Showing in Turkish the literal, incidental, figurative, colloquial, and technical significations of the English Terms: preceded by a Sketch of English Etymology. Royal 8vo. pp. 844, printed with very small but singularly clear types, both the English and the Turkish, half-bound red morocco, new, 24s. 1861

A singularly well-executed work, offered at less than half the rate of production. The low price is due to the generosity of William Wheelright, Esq. of Newburyport, U.S.A., who defrayed all the expenses of authorship and printing. A few copies of Redhouse's Turkish-English Dictionary, 1 vol. 8vo. remain, price 15s.: this vol. will serve as a counterpart to the above.

Redhouse's Turkish Dictionary.

In Two Parts. Part 1, English and Turkish; Part 2, Turkish-English; in which the Turkish words are represented in the Oriental character, as well as their correct pronunciation and accentuation shown in English letters. By J. W. REDHOUSE, F.R.S.A., Member of the Imperial Academy of Science of Constantinople, &c. In 1 stout vol. small square 8vo. pp. 1177 (published at £2), cloth, 30s. 1857

*** The first English and Turkish Dictionary published. Not a dozen copies remain for sale.

Barker's Turkish Grammar, Dialogues and Vocabulary.

A Practical Guide to the Acquisition of the Turkish Language. 1 vol. 12mo. pp. 166, cloth, 4s. 1854